Faithful biblical exposition that is Spirit-led is a must for healthy churches. Such preaching will enlighten the mind and feed the soul. *Spirit-Led Preaching* by Greg Heisler is a wonderful treatment of the role of the Spirit in gospel proclamation. This is a must addition to the library of any pastor who recognizes his need for supernatural enablement in teaching the Word of God.

Daniel L. Akin
President, Southeastern Baptist Theological Seminary

Only the Holy Spirit can deliver a sermon from ineffectiveness. This book pierces to the heart of the issue of what makes preaching truly powerful. Only faithful exposition of the Scripture coupled with a firm reliance upon the Holy Spirit will truly produce life transformation. The man-centered circus of so much that goes under the banner of being "anointed" these days is effectively countered by Heisler, who tells us why and how we can learn to prepare sermons saturated with the Holy Spirit and preach them dependent upon the Holy Spirit's power. If you want to learn about the Holy Spirit's ministry in your preaching, get this book.

David L. Allen
Professor of Preaching
Dean, Director of the Southwestern Center for Expository Preaching
George W. Truett Chair of Ministry
Southwestern Baptist Theological Seminary

The great reformers of the sixteenth century emphasized the indispensable linkage and coinherence of Word and Spirit in the life of the church. This book clearly presses that point home with reference to the central task of proclamation. In an age marked by frenzy on the one hand and lethargy on the other, we need a revival of the kind of preaching called for in this book—God honoring, Christ centered, Spirit anointed, soul searching, passionate, convicting, and courageous. May God give us heralds of the gospel who preach like this!

Timothy George
Dean, Beeson Divinity School, Samford University
Executive Editor, Christianity Today

Biblical preaching is the communication of God's truth in a relevant manner through the personification of a man empowered by the Holy Spirit. This empowerment comes publicly to the degree it has been endowed privately in that preacher's personal life and devotion before Jesus daily. This book challenges us to wrestle with this need not only in our preaching but also in our personal lives. This endowment by the Spirit of God is needed upon us as communicators of God's Word. Before I ~~~~~ ~~~~ Sunday, I kneel and pray into my life 1 Corinthians 2:4–5. I am n ... ıd I know it. Before I leave my chair in the aı ... God personally for the anointing of the Holy ... ı calling us to Holy

D1114143

Spirit-led preparation, planning, and presentation. I believe you are meeting an outstanding need for all of us.

Ronnie W. Floyd
Pastor, First Baptist Church, Springdale, Arkansas

An old hymn reminds us that "all is vain unless the Spirit of the Holy One comes down!" Indeed, effective preaching requires the Holy Spirit. He is the One who (1) inspired the Scriptures, (2) saves, calls, and equips the preacher, and (3) convicts, convinces, and converts the listener. In his new book *Spirit-Led Preaching*, Dr. Greg Heisler shows us how and why the Holy Spirit should superintend each aspect of preaching from the study to the pulpit. I highly recommend this work to those who seek more divine power in their preaching!

Steve Gaines
Senior Pastor, Bellevue Baptist Church
Memphis, Tennessee

I feel that we all could agree that there is no greater need in our preaching than the touch of God. Dr. Greg Heisler has done us all a great service in that he has written this book with the Holy Spirit's role in Spirit-led preaching in mind. I am grateful for every resource that I can study for the illumination of God's Spirit in opening up the text, but I have found that the greatest need is for God's touch by His precious Holy Spirit in delivery of that message. This book will keep that in the forefront of your mind. Read it, and recommend this book to others.

Pastor Johnny Hunt
First Baptist Church
Woodstock, Georgia

Compare Ephesians 5:18–19 with Colossians 3:16 and a remarkable truth emerges. Scripture equates Spirit-filled living with letting the Word of Christ dwell richly within. That is precisely the key to authentic Spirit-empowered preaching, too. When prominence is given to the Word of God rather than to the antics of the preacher or the feelings of the hearers, that is when preaching is most Spirit directed. Greg Heisler has wonderfully traced the New Testament theme of the Holy Spirit's role in our preaching. Greg's passion for Spirit-led preaching is contagious; his insights are both wise and biblical; and this book should therefore be a great help and encouragement to any preacher who longs for the Spirit's true anointing in the pulpit.

John MacArthur
Pastor, Grace Community Church

In this day of "give them what they want," Greg Heisler sounds a clarion call for God's messengers to "give them what they need," which is a Holy Spirit-appointed preacher delivering a Holy Spirit-anointed message from a Holy Spirit-inspired Bible! This book will help all of us who have the calling of God to preach

His truth to lift our message from being just a word for God to being a word *from* God—infused with the power that can only come from above.

James Merritt
Pastor, Crosse Point, The Church at Gwinnett Church
Duluth, Georgia

At its heart, preaching is a supernatural activity that can be accomplished only through the work of the Holy Spirit. In *Spirit-Led Preaching*, Greg Heisler provides a much-needed biblical model for sermons and preachers that are authentically empowered by the Spirit of Holy God. This book is for all preachers who hunger and thirst for the fullest power of God upon their pulpit ministry.

Stephen N. Rummage
Preaching Pastor, Hickory Grove Baptist Church
Charlotte, North Carolina

One of the greatest hazards in preaching is to overlook the Spirit's role. Dr. Heisler's excellent book drives home the truth that the Spirit is vital in every aspect of preaching. His emphasis on the fusion of the Word and Spirit in preaching is the antidote for what ails the modern pulpit. If you desire to preach in demonstration of the Spirit's power, *Spirit-Led Preaching* outlines the biblical roadmap.

Timothy C. Seal
Chairman, Department of Practical Theology
Associate Dean of the Adrian Rogers Center for Biblical Preaching
Mid-America Baptist Theological Seminary

Dr. Heisler has contributed a much-needed volume to the field of sermon preparation and delivery. The role of the Holy Spirit in preparing messages and then delivering them is much neglected in the literature, and I fear, in the actual process of the preaching experience. Dr. Heisler brings us back to what Paul surely intended when he said that preaching should be "in demonstration of the Spirit and power" (1 Cor. 2:4). Read this book and be blessed and challenged.

Jerry Vines
Pastor Emeritus
First Baptist Church, Jacksonville, Florida

Many who hear evangelicals talk today about preaching would be surprised to hear us talk about Scripture without the Holy Spirit. That is because the church through the centuries has understood the combined gift of Spirit and Word that is to culminate in the preaching event. Greg Heisler has written an important book that will help to educate a new generation of evangelicals about the power of preaching through the Holy Spirit and the Word.

R. Albert Mohler Jr.
President, The Southern Baptist Theological Seminary

The great movements of God throughout history have always been marked by three catalysts: God's people prayed, God's preachers preached, and the Spirit of God moved! Greg Heisler's book captures the dynamic relationship between the Word of God, the Spirit of God, and the preacher of God. With such a strong emphasis on preaching Christ, this book uniquely brings together a passion for preaching and a passion for the lost that will challenge the hearts of those who read it.

Alvin Reid
Bailey Smith Professor of Evangelism
Southeastern Baptist Theological Seminary

The great need of the hour is for a strong expositional pulpit. Greg Heisler provides us with a solid resource that is soundly based in the practice of expositional hermeneutics with the Spirit's help. This will help pastors with the steps that lead to responsible exegesis and powerful preaching.

Mac Brunson
Pastor, First Baptist Church, Dallas, Texas

While books on preaching focus on writing and presenting the sermon, too often they overlook the key factor upon which preaching stands and falls: the inspiration and empowering of the Holy Spirit. Greg Heisler has taken on this vital subject and offers a helpful exploration of the vital work of the Holy Spirit in the faithful proclamation of God's Word.

Michael Duduit
Editor, Preaching *magazine*

Greg Heisler has presided over the wedding of the preacher's preparation and the Spirit's power. He demonstrates that we need have no conflict between passionate delivery and pietistic devotion, nor need we choose between intellect and anointing. Whether the preacher is at his desk in intense study or on his knees in intense supplication, his most desperate need is the enabling power of the Holy Spirit. Heisler's book saves us from the extremes of a cold rationalism and a mindless emotionalism and teaches us how to find the divine balance of Word and Spirit. My heart has long waited for this book.

Hershael W. York
Victor and Louise Lester Professor of Christian Preaching
Southern Baptist Theological Seminary

SPIRIT-LED
Preaching

SPIRIT-LED
Preaching

The Holy Spirit's Role in
Sermon Preparation and Delivery

GREG HEISLER

NASHVILLE, TENNESSEE

ISBN: 978-0-8054-4388-2

Published by B&H Publishing Group
Nashville, Tennessee

Dewey Decimal Classification: 231.3
Subject Heading: HOLY SPIRIT \ PREACHING

6 7 8 9 10 11 12 • 15 14 13 12 11 10

V

To Laura,
my bride, my love, and my support.
To Andrew and Benjamin,
the arrows God has blessed
us with (Ps. 127:4).

To Danny Akin and Robert Smith Jr.,
the two men who took me in as a young Timothy,
and helped me become a better preacher
but more importantly showed me what it means to be a man
after God's own heart.

Contents

Foreword

In the fall of 1995 at The Southern Baptist Theological Seminary in Louisville, Kentucky, a young man in one of my classes preached a sermon from Revelation 1:17–18, a text that showcases the glorified Christ, who was resurrected by the power of the Holy Spirit. Little did I know that that young man, Greg Heisler, would experience a call to preach—not on a Damascus road like Paul, not in a winepress like Gideon, not while picking sycamore fruit like Amos, and not while lying in bed like Samuel but rather, in my homiletics classroom. God used the words of the apostle Paul, "Woe to me, if I do not preach the gospel," to pierce his heart with unceasing and overwhelming prophetic burden to preach the Word.

It has been my magnanimous privilege to watch God use him as he has progressed from a call to preach to a call to pastor to his most recent call to serve as a seminary professor at Southeastern Seminary in Wake Forest, North Carolina. His book *Spirit-Led Preaching* is a much needed and timely work in the field of homiletics. The Christian church is quick to emphasize the importance of Spirit-led singing, Spirit-led praying, and Spirit-led living. However, there has been a long and overdue promulgation on the necessity of Spirit-led preaching.

The contemporary church suffers from the ache of memory that has resulted in pneumatological amputation and absence. In fact, the Holy Spirit has been demoted to the status of the stepchild of the Trinity, especially in preaching. A plethora of noted preachers join in a chorus of ecclesiastical indictment on the church for demoting the importance of the work of the Holy Spirit in the life of the church. James Forbes in his 1989 book *The Holy Spirit and Preaching* indicts the church for being "Holy Spirit shy." Stephen Olford in his work *Spirit-Anointed Expository Preaching* says that the sin of the Old Testament was the rejection of God the Father, the sin of the New Testament was a rejection of God the Son, and the sin of the contemporary church is the rejection of God the Spirit.

C. H. Dodd in his 1936 watershed work *The Apostolic Preaching and Its Development* lists six elements of the *kerygma,* the gospel message of the early apostles. The fifth element is *metanoia*—repentance accompanied by the Holy Spirit, as evidenced in Acts 2:38: "Repent and be baptized, every one of you, in the name of Jesus Christ for the forgiveness of your sins. And you will receive the gift of the Holy Spirit." Ecclesiastical prophet A. W. Tozer surmised that if God decided to take the Holy Spirit out of the church, the church after twenty-five years would still be doing the same thing and not even notice the difference!

Even Jesus, who had the Holy Spirit without measure and is the human face of God—God with skin, representing God without skin—who would send the Holy Spirit to be God inside *our* skin, said in his inaugural sermon in Nazareth: "The Spirit of the Lord is upon me, for he has anointed me to preach good news to the poor" (Luke 4:18). If Jesus the Son of God, the infinite One, the sender of the Holy Spirit to the church on the day of Pentecost, declared that the Spirit of the Lord was upon Him to preach, can we preachers, who are frail, weak, and finite vessels, settle for anything less? To see the work of God demonstrated in our preaching necessitates the indwelling power of the Holy Spirit.

In these days of unprecedented fear and incomparable tragedies, the Spirit and the Word need to be married together in an inextricable bond so that the hearers of our gospel can be initiated into the faith through the gospel, instructed by the faith through the gospel, and inspired to keep the faith through the gospel.

Dr. Heisler reminds us in this work that preaching carries a dual responsibility: It is the hand of the human preacher and the hand of God through the Holy Spirit that makes preaching effective. His work is an epitome of Augustine's contention that we ought to work as if everything depended on us and pray as if everything depended on God. The book bridges the gap between the head and the heart, what other homileticians like Fred Craddock call "the longest journey in the world."

Dr. Heisler reminds us that preaching is not a planned and calculated event accomplished through mere human preparation, but rather it is an inexplicable and supernatural happening executed by the power of the Holy Spirit through the human agency of the preacher. To paraphrase the well-known definition of preaching provided by Phillips Brooks, preaching is the truth of God mediated and poured through the personality of the preacher by the power of the Holy Spirit.

Haddon Robinson, professor of preaching at Gordon Conwell Theological Seminary, includes in his definition of biblical preaching that after the textual idea is discerned through a grammatical, historical, and literary study of a passage in its context, that the Holy Spirit must first apply the text to the life and personality of the preacher and then to the hearers. This is precisely the focus of Dr. Heisler's book, and his challenge to us is to be Spirit-filled Christians before we are Spirit-empowered preachers.

This book is a success waiting to happen. I congratulate my son in the faith, Dr. Heisler, for ushering us as readers into the real presence of Christ and for urging us who preach the Scriptures to make Christ's presence real in every sermon. May the great "after preacher"—the Holy Spirit—provide not only the manner but the matter for the declaration of the whole counsel of God, to the end that every knee will bow and every tongue confess that Jesus is Lord.

To God be the glory—great things He hath done.

Robert Smith Jr.
Professor of Preaching
Beeson Divinity School
Birmingham, Alabama

Preface

In 1980, Haddon Robinson's *Biblical Preaching* challenged evangelical preachers to recover the centrality of the biblical text for preaching, and as a result a renaissance of expository preaching began. For far too long the needs and demands of the biblical text had been neglected, and Robinson's book launched what I believe to be a reformation of Christian preaching. Throughout the 1980s and 1990s, more advocates of expository preaching such as John MacArthur, Stephen Olford, John Stott, and Bryan Chappell arose; and many seminaries placed a new emphasis on expository preaching, some even offering advanced degrees in the field. The reformation in preaching was clearly a move back to the text, and as a result the expository sermon experienced a "resurrection" in homiletics.

Due to the resurgence of expository preaching, students in seminaries and Bible colleges often hear their homiletics professor say, "It's the text! It's the text that drives the sermon—interpret the text, explain the text, apply the text!" As a student and practitioner of expository preaching, I affirm wholeheartedly the centrality of the text in the development and proclamation of a sermon. Our handling of the biblical text does matter, and we must exposit God's Word through careful exegesis coupled with a holy reverence for the task God has called us to as preachers of the Word of the living God!

I do not believe the reformation of Christian preaching, specifically expository preaching, is complete. In addition to a strong emphasis on the text of Scripture, we must place an equally strong emphasis on the Holy Spirit who empowers us to preach the Scriptures. The resurgence of expository preaching has lacked a fresh and substantive look at the Spirit's role in expository preaching. We can no longer be shy of the Spirit's work in preaching. We need both the Spirit and the Word in order to proclaim the Scriptures powerfully.

As much as preaching today needs the authority of God's Word, it also needs the power of the Holy Spirit. In addition to our strong emphasis on the text of Scripture, we must place an equally strong emphasis on the Holy Spirit, who empowers us to preach the

Scriptures. The resurgence of expository preaching has lacked a fresh and substantive look at the Spirit's role in preaching. We cannot separate the Word from the Spirit or the Spirit from the Word; we need both the Spirit and the Word to powerfully proclaim the Scriptures.

Spirit-Led Preaching: The Holy Spirit's Role in Sermon Preparation and Delivery is a call issued to preachers, pastors, and teachers of homiletics to recover the Holy Spirit for expository preaching in the same way we have recovered the biblical text. My hope and prayer is that we will approach the role of the Spirit in preaching with as much zeal and as much fervor as we have the biblical text. In our boldness to return preaching to the biblical text, I believe we have unintentionally marginalized the ministry of the Holy Spirit, making the Spirit secondary to the needs of the text. For many preachers the Holy Spirit is relegated to the background of preaching, working behind the scenes, assumed but not readily understood. My intention in this book is to move the Spirit to the foreground of our preaching where his role in preaching is more clearly understood and more deeply depended upon. My plan for doing this is to recover the doctrine of pneumatology for our theology of preaching, resulting in a renewed emphasis on the powerful combination of Word and Spirit working together as the catalyst of all transformational preaching.

The recovery of the Holy Spirit's role in expository preaching will enrich and empower our preaching and our churches. Not only will students and practitioners of preaching understand the mechanics of the text, but they will also be conversant and experienced in the dynamics of the Spirit. Instead of only hearing, "The text, the text, the text," in their homiletic classrooms, they will start hearing, "The text and the Spirit, the Spirit and the text—the Word of God and the Spirit of God." Our strong emphasis on preaching the Word of God will be matched with an equal dependence upon the Spirit of God. Our bibliology will be wonderfully complemented by our pneumatology, and the result will be powerful preaching that changes lives for all eternity—nothing less than "a demonstration of the Spirit's power" (1 Cor. 2:4).

Greg W. Heisler
Wake Forest, North Carolina

Introduction

What Spirit-Empowered Preaching Looks Like

I can't measure it. I can't quantify it. I can't feel it. I don't know what it is the Holy Spirit is doing; I don't know when He's doing it and when He's not. In fact, I've said this, but there are times when you feel . . . you know this, there's a great freedom when you preach and you feel like something's kind of carrying you along and you're better than you should be, right? And you just feel like it was cohesive and it came together and it worked. . . . He illumines the Word to my mind, and empowers my passion.

—*John MacArthur, Shepherd's Conference, 2005*

Everybody needs a hero. My childhood hero of choice was Superman—faster than a speeding bullet, more powerful than a locomotive. It's a bird. It's a plane. It's _____! I think the transformation of mild-mannered Clark Kent into the bold and courageous Superman was something everyone could identify with. Judging from outward appearances, Clark Kent wasn't much to contend with. But we all knew what was underneath that shirt and tie. The "S" on his chest stood for the true power inside him.

Do preachers have a hidden *S* underneath their ministerial garb—not an *S* pointing to their superhuman strength but an *S* pointing to the supernatural power of the Holy Spirit? Does the Holy Spirit still empower preachers today? If so, how? Do we pray and study throughout our week like a Clark Kent, only to change into blue tights and a red cape on Sunday morning in hopeful expectation of something supernatural happening? Or do we begin our sermons as the mild-mannered Clark Kent, waiting expectantly for the Spirit to miraculously transform us at some point of the message into Superman, so we can fly out of the pulpit at high noon every week?

"Nonsense," you may be saying to yourself, "preachers are just human beings like everybody else." Yet in a 2004 Knight Ridder news article on the Holy Spirit, one evangelical pastor had this to say about the role of the Holy Spirit in Christian's life: "We are Clark Kent, but with the Holy Spirit, we become Superman."

When I read a statement like that, immediately my childhood images of Superman come to mind: able to bend steel bars with his bare hands, able to see through walls with X-ray vision, able to lift massive objects with superhuman strength, able to leap tall buildings with a single bound, faster than a speeding bullet, more powerful than a locomotive. It's a bird; it's a plane; it's . . . a Spirit-filled Christian? Talk of Christians turning into Superman via the power of the Holy Spirit may fit well with a culture obsessed with extreme makeovers, but it certainly has no foundation in Scripture. In fact, Paul's self-assessment as a God-called, Spirit-filled preacher of the gospel stands in stark contrast to any Superman mentality: "I came to you in weakness and in fear, and with much trembling" (1 Cor. 2:3).

Paul doesn't sound like Superman, does he? Yet in the next verse Paul affirms that underneath all his trembling and weakness, his preaching donned the *S*—not of Superman but of the Holy Spirit: "My message and my preaching were not with wise and persuasive words, but with a demonstration of the Spirit's power, so that your faith might not rest on men's wisdom [not even Superman's!], but on God's power" (1 Cor. 2:4). Paul acknowledges that his powerful preaching is not from anything within himself; he plainly tells the Corinthians there is nothing special about him: "What, after all, is Apollos? And what is Paul? Only servants" (1 Cor. 3:5). It seems the Holy Spirit turned Paul into a servant rather than a Superman, and a weak one at that.

Furthermore, I cannot recall Superman boasting about his inherent weakness to kryptonite. To do so would lessen his superhero image. In contrast Paul not only admits his weaknesses; he *boasts* in them! "Therefore I will boast all the more gladly about my weaknesses, so that Christ's power may rest on me. That is why, for Christ's sake, I delight in weaknesses, in insults, in hardships, in persecutions, in difficulties. For when I am weak, then I am strong" (2 Cor. 12:9).

Judging from the verses quoted above, Paul doesn't sound like a superhero at all. Yet no honest reader of the New Testament would deny the power of God that accompanied Paul's ministry of the Word. As pastors today, we live in a church culture filled with large egos, supersized pride, and superhero expectations—pressures the man of steel himself could not handle! Yet we must reject any notion that we are Superman called to be a superhero. The hero of our preaching is Jesus Christ, and our goal as preachers is to be Spirit filled and Spirit empowered so that our audience knows the difference between supernatural preaching and superhero preaching! Preaching is not an exhibition of the Superman skills you may have learned in seminary or at a seminar; rather, as Paul says, it is a demonstration of the Spirit's power. If we know we want to end up with preaching that is Spirit-empowered, the question remains, "What path do we take to get there?"

As preachers we are quick to confess the need for the Spirit's power in our preaching, but we fall short when it comes to explaining *how* to involve the Holy Spirit in our preaching. The fruit of evangelical publishing and scholarship over the last two decades demonstrates that as evangelicals we are far more able to tell what the Spirit *does not do* in preaching as opposed to what the Spirit *must do* if powerful proclamation is to take place. My conviction is that we have failed to connect the discipline of homiletics with the doctrine of pneumatology, and as a result we find ourselves "surprised by the Spirit" when he does move. *Spirit-Led Preaching* seeks to establish a positive theology of the Spirit's role in preaching by building upon the theological fusion of Word and Spirit.

The Purpose and Plan of Spirit-Led Preaching

The premise upon which *Spirit-Led Preaching* is based is this: if Spirit-empowered sermons are going to be preached, then a Spirit-led approach to preaching must be followed. *Spirit-Led Preaching* is more about a mind-set than a method. It is directed toward keeping our hearts aligned with the Spirit, rather than just keeping our outlines in line with the same letter. Our sermon preparation and sermon delivery must be intentionally and prayerfully carried out under the leadership and power of the Holy Spirit. In order to accomplish this, the preacher must come to see preaching as the Spirit's ministry, not the preacher's own ministry. The Spirit is the one who does the preaching through the proclamation of the Word. God by his grace uses us—personalities and all—to spread the good news of Jesus Christ. The preacher who is Spirit driven, Spirit led, and Spirit dependent will also be Spirit empowered! Preaching is truly the Spirit's ministry. Just think of how many ways the Spirit is involved in preaching:

Ten Ways the Holy Spirit Is at Work in Preaching

1. The Spirit's inspiration of the biblical text
2. The conversion of the preacher to faith in Jesus Christ
3. The call of the preacher to preach the Word
4. The character of the preacher to live the Word
5. The illumination of the preacher's heart and mind in study
6. The empowerment of the preacher in proclaiming the Word
7. The testimony to Jesus Christ as Lord and mediator
8. The opening of the hearts of those who hear and receive the Word
9. The application of the Word of God to the listeners' lives
10. The production of lasting fruit displayed in the lives of Spirit-filled believers

---

Spirit-Led Preaching is designed to help preachers see just how much of preaching is influenced by the Holy Spirit. In chapters 1 through 5, I build the theological foundation for Spirit-led preaching by examining the biblical, hermeneutical, and theological foundations regarding preaching and the Spirit. In chapters 6 through 9, I address the practical implications of Spirit-led preaching.

Preaching is an act of surrender. In our humble brokenness before God, we are compelled to carry out our preaching ministry under the unceasing inner compulsion of the Holy Spirit. The most powerful preaching on earth comes out of a preacher who *must* say what he has to say. Spirit-led preaching does not result from our own strength or power but from God's power as the Holy Spirit energizes and ignites the preaching of his Word.

I think Spirit-led preaching captures well the dynamic relationship between the preacher, the Spirit, and the Word. According to Luke 4, Jesus was "led by the Spirit" (v. 1), "returned in the power of the Spirit" (v. 14), and then was "anointed by the Spirit to preach" (v. 18). The word *led* in verse 1 literally means "to lead by taking hold of." The word carries with it the idea of force or power and is translated elsewhere "to move, to compel, to urge, and to direct." The idea for preaching is clear: Spirit-led preaching is preaching that is birthed and delivered by the powerful moving of the Spirit so that the Spirit takes hold of us and compels us to preach. Spirit-led preaching is accomplished by a preacher who in his surrendered state has been "taken hold of" by the Spirit. As the Spirit takes hold of the preacher and compels him to preach, the Spirit also takes hold of the audience and compels them to listen, and God speaks.

The book unfolds in the following manner. In chapter 1 I look at the absence of the Holy Spirit in preaching and give some explanations as to why we don't emphasize the Spirit in preaching. In chapter 2 I define preaching in terms of the Spirit, highlighting the Spirit's biblical ministries that form the basis of Spirit-led preaching. In chapter 3 I present the biblical evidence for Spirit-led preaching by examining Old Testament prophetic preaching and New Testament Pauline preaching. In chapter 4 I make the case for a recovery of the illumination of the Holy Spirit for preaching and will clarify the Spirit's role between an inspired text and an illumined interpreter. In chapter 5 I make the case that Spirit-led preaching must implement a proper theology of Word and Spirit.

Chapter 6 begins the practical application by discussing how the Spirit influences the preacher's conversion, call, training, and character. Chapter 7 turns to the preacher's preparation of the sermon under the Spirit's leadership, noting that what the Spirit illumines in the study, he empowers in the pulpit. Chapter 8 covers the practical issues of sermon delivery and emphasizes the three-way conversation that takes place during preaching between the preacher, the congregation, and the Holy Spirit. Finally, chapter 9 addresses the Spirit's empowerment for preaching popularly referred to as the anointing.

Before we begin, I want to let you know up front what this book is not intended to be or do. This book is not intended to be a how-to introduction to sermon preparation. This book is intended to be read alongside those books, to remind you that the Holy Spirit is preparing you to preach as you prepare to preach his text! Nor is this book a call to practice mysticism or illuminism, or to seek special revelations or other types of extrabiblical experiences. The book is very much grounded in the biblical doctrines of revelation and pneumatology.

My hope is that Spirit-led preaching will cause you to approach your own preaching with a heightened sensitivity to the Spirit's leadership. I pray that the book will cause you to become more holistic in your approach to preaching and will foster in you a fresh dependence upon the Spirit in your life and in your preaching ministry. The book will succeed if it causes you to be more sensitive to the Spirit's dynamic role in your preaching. To take a stand on the Word of God is to take a stand for the Spirit of God who inspired it. To preach the Word is to honor the Spirit, and to honor the Spirit is to preach his Word. Homiletics shall not separate what God has joined together!

Just as every kid needs a hero, so every preacher needs the Holy Spirit. Although we are not called to be a Superman in the pulpit, we are called to be servants—servants of the Word of God, under the empowerment of the Spirit of God, and all for the glory of God. So the next time you get up to preach, remember this: there is an unseen *S* that accompanies you to the pulpit. No, the *S* is not written across your chest; it is written deep upon your heart and sealed upon your soul. It stands for the Spirit—the Holy Spirit.

Chapter 1

Missing in Action:
Where Is the Holy Spirit
When We Preach?

*Our generation is rapidly losing its grip upon the
supernatural; and as a consequence, the pulpit is
rapidly dropping to the level of the platform. And this
decline is due, more than anything else, to ignoring the
Holy Spirit as the supreme inspirer of preaching. We
would rather see a great orator in the pulpit, forgetting
that the least expounder of the Word, when filled with
the Spirit, is greater than he.*

—A. J. Gordon

I can still remember the conversation to this day: "Preacher, all
these people haven't come today to hear you preach. I know it's
Sunday morning and it's church, but they're not interested in
hearing preaching today. They want to hear the music group sing, not
hear you preach." Those were shocking words to a young pastor with
his heart set on preaching the Word of God and winning the world
for Jesus Christ. As this older deacon lectured me on what really
mattered to the congregation on such a special day (no preaching
= more music), I found my mind drifting back to Romans 10:14
where Paul says, "How, then, can they call on the one they have not
believed in? And how can they believe in the one of whom they have
not heard? And how can they hear without someone preaching to

them?" Hearing music is one thing. But hearing the Word of God proclaimed, Paul says, is essential to bringing people to saving faith in Jesus Christ.

I have nothing against great music in a church worship service; in fact, more often than not, it warms and stirs my heart before I preach. I also have nothing against using the arts in worship. Readings, dramas, and visuals can enhance our worship experience. What I am dead-set against is allowing all these "good things" to crowd out and push out the "most needed thing"—the preaching of the Word! What that deacon was sharing with me opened my eyes to a stark reality and a growing trend I have seen among churches today: Preaching is no longer the priority of the church.

The Contemporary Setting

Preaching has once again fallen on hard times. From a postmodern perspective, preaching is seen by many as rationalistic, elitist, and authoritarian. In a culture that worships at the altar of relativism and idolizes ideas that do not offend anyone, there is little tolerance for any preacher to be so bold as to proclaim, "Thus says the Lord." Cultural critic and theologian Al Mohler believes biblical preaching has been replaced with needs-based, human-centered approaches to avoid what he calls "a potentially embarrassing confrontation with biblical truth."[1] John Piper laments the decline of faithful biblical exposition in the face of a changing culture when he observes how preaching has become "relational, anecdotal, humorous, casual, laid-back, absorbed in human need, fixed on relational dynamics, heavily saturated with psychological categories, and wrapped up in strategies for emotional healing."[2]

Preaching has lost its theological mandate. Consequently, we have replaced preachers with speakers because we are told people want dialogue without doctrine and talks without truth. Theology is out, storytellers are in, and as a result we are seeing an entire generation

---

1. Al Mohler, "The Urgency of Preaching," Weblog 25 June 2004. Available at www. crosswalk.com/news/weblogs/mohler.

2. John Piper, "Preaching as Worship: Meditations on Expository Exultation," *Trinity Journal* 16 (Spring 1995): 30.

of preachers who are more driven to be effective communicators than to be Spirit-empowered preachers. Methodology trumps theology, and sensitivity to the audience has replaced sensitivity to the Spirit.

Even those who propose expository preaching as the cure to the ailments of preaching today are not always preaching expository sermons; and when they do preach them, they do not preach them in an engaging manner. Poorly preached sermons, no matter what kind they are, give preaching a black eye. My first experience with preaching came through Young Life, a youth ministry that seeks to impact teenagers with the gospel. When it was my turn to give the message, my leader told me, "Never forget cardinal rule number one: It's a sin to bore people with the gospel of Jesus Christ!" If you are a preacher or preparing to be a preacher, let me challenge you right now to take a moment to pray, and determine in your heart today that if people come to church and leave bored, it will not be because of your preaching! I tell my students in my preaching classes, "If you are boring in the pulpit today, it's no one's fault but your own."

Let's face the facts for a moment. We have more commentaries today than we know what to do with or have time to read, so understanding the text should not be the problem. We have access to millions of illustrations with Google and the Web. We have entire Web sites dedicated to helping us preach, and we have powerful computer software that can exegete the Hebrew and Greek text for us at the click of a mouse. Even when it comes to delivery, we have programs like PowerPoint to help us present our message in a visually stimulating way. We are spoiled indeed! So why, even with all these wonderful tools and technologies, do our sermons come across as boring, uninteresting, irrelevant, and uninspiring?

Could it be that the most important ingredient to engaging and powerful preaching cannot be boxed up and sold on a shelf or downloaded from the Web? Could it be that the reason our sermons are so passionless and powerless today is not that we lack resources but that we lack power—supernatural power? Yes, we have made ourselves more efficient, but has the Spirit made our messages more powerful?

Our calling as preachers is to proclaim the Bible, plain and simple. We must also deliver God's Word in an engaging and authentic manner. My conviction is that the Spirit of God and the Word of God come together in the heart and mind of the preacher to produce substantive and compelling sermons that transform the lives of listeners. A preacher's head and heart must meet together in the Holy Spirit to produce powerful preaching that informs the mind, inflames the heart, moves the will, and transforms the life. The Word of God is the substance of our message. It is living and active, sharper than any two-edged sword (Heb. 4:12). The Spirit of God is the fire of our message. He ignites us as we prepare it and deliver it, and he ignites our listeners as they hear it!

One way to overcome the apathy of the pew toward preaching is for preachers to return to the days of Jeremiah, when the Word of God was so powerfully shut up in his bones like fire that he couldn't hold it in (Jer. 20:9)! Come to the pulpit so full of the Word of God and so full of the Spirit of God—unable to hold it in—and you will find that your people cannot wait to take it in! Moody said, "Catch on fire for Jesus, and the world will come and watch you burn."

What's the Solution?

Why have so many churches been unaffected by the ministry of the Word? I believe the answer lies in our failure to harness the synergistic power that results when the Spirit of God and the Word of God combine together in preaching. We have so emphasized the needs of the text—and those are crucial needs indeed—that the Spirit's contribution to preaching seems secondary at best. We forget that without the Spirit we would have no text to begin with and without the Spirit we would have no illumined heart to discern the text (1 Cor. 2:14). Nothing short of a renaissance of the Holy Spirit's role in preaching will save powerless pulpits and sick churches from ineffective kingdom ministry.

In this book I am not advocating replacing the emphasis on the Word with an emphasis on the Spirit. I am advocating adding the Spirit's emphasis to the present emphasis on preaching the Word. I think A. J. Gordon's assessment is right. We have lost our sense of the supernatural, and as a result preaching has become the activity of man instead of the ministry of God.

Whatever Happened to the Holy Spirit?

Where did we get offtrack with regard to the supernatural—especially the Holy Spirit's involvement in preaching? Unfortunately, explanations are scarce and answers are few and far between. First of all, most textbooks on preaching have little to say about the Spirit. Even classic preaching texts like John Broadus's *On the Preparation and Delivery of Sermons* have little to say about the Spirit in preaching. A generation of preachers in the 1930s and 1940s were raised on Andrew Blackwood's preaching texts, which also place little emphasis on the Spirit's involvement in preaching. In fact, the broad consensus of the literature as a whole reveals little interest in the Spirit. Only recently, with the publication of books like Jerry Vines and Jim Shaddix's *Power in the Pulpit* (1999), as well as Stephen Olford and David Olford's *Anointed Expository Preaching* (1998), have textbooks on how to prepare a sermon incorporated more than a passing reference to the Spirit.

Preaching Definitions

One of the most obvious omissions of the Spirit's role in preaching is seen in how rare it is to find the Spirit incorporated into a definition of preaching. This is ironic since the way you define something will ultimately determine the outcome you can expect. In general, preaching definitions tend to center on the preacher, the Bible, and the delivery. Yet if preaching is the Spirit's ministry and if the final goal of our preaching is a demonstration of the Spirit's power, then we must define preaching to encompass the rich theology of Word and Spirit from the very beginning. In the next chapter I will develop the Spirit-led definition of preaching used throughout the rest of the book.

What does the Spirit's absence from the definitions of preaching reveal to us? First, I believe it shows just how post-theological preaching has become. Contemporary preaching begins with the audience instead of God, and as a result preaching has become the trade of communicators, not pastor-theologians. Many preaching books, Web sites, and preaching blogs focus heavily on the pragmatic side of preaching by emphasizing techniques, tips, mechanics, and the how-to approach to preaching. Don't get me wrong; we need to learn the pragmatic side of preaching because the techniques and mechanical elements of preaching do help us to become better preachers. My concern is that often these books, Web sites, and blogs tell only half the story of what preaching is all about. We need to know how to put a sermon together, but before we tackle the how-tos, let's first learn the "why-do" by establishing the theological foundation and spiritual dynamic of preaching.

Put another way, sound mechanics must be complemented by spiritual dynamics lest we end up with a Rolls Royce sermon that looks great on paper but has no gas in the tank to give it any power. In *Spirit-Led Preaching* I am calling for a more holistic and theologically driven approach to preaching that by definition and design incorporates the dynamic Spirit of God ministering the living Word of God through the Spirit-empowered man of God. The Spirit adds the homiletic gas to the preacher's tank, empowering the sermon and ensuring that our preaching goes someplace!

Spirit-Led Preaching is *intentionally* centered on the theological and spiritual *dynamics* of preaching while still maintaining the importance of good sermon *mechanics*. This means that our sermons can have clear structure and can be Spirit-filled at the same time. Some preachers do not believe you can have the Spirit and structure at the same time because for them being led by the Spirit in preaching means unpredictability, and man-made structures tend to get in the way of the unpredictable and unstructured Spirit! In this view any sermon with clarity and sound structure is decried as man's creation not the Spirit's.

Yet when we begin to think about the Spirit's work of inspiration, we would not conclude that the Spirit-inspired Word of God has no structure, would we? Of course not! The Bible is replete with structure because the Spirit's inspiration was captured in words, which were placed into sentences, which were combined into coherent paragraphs, which fit into the flow of the writer's overall argument, and so on. So the Spirit can and does work within good, clear sermon structure, especially if that structure is shaped by and anchored to the biblical text.

Is there a danger in having sound sermon structure and good preaching mechanics? Yes, the danger we face as preachers comes in the form of a misplaced confidence. For example, when I begin to think that the power and effectiveness of my sermon comes from how well-structured or how well-packaged my sermon is on a given Sunday, I will quench and grieve the true power of preaching—the Holy Spirit of God. As a preacher of God's Word, I must constantly remind myself that the power of my sermon is not located in how well my outline comes together in alliterative fashion. The power of my sermon does not come from the balanced symmetry and parallelism of my three points and my three subpoints. The power of my sermon does not come from my creative introduction or my perfect-fitting illustration. The preached message always finds its true source of power in the theological fusion of the Word of God and the Spirit of God joining together in Christological witness to the Son of God, coming through the proclamation of the man of God.

The Holy Spirit and Shyness

A second reason for the Spirit's absence in preaching today has to do with the excesses and abuses attributed to the Spirit. Everything from laughing, crying, barking like a dog, meowing like a cat, passing out at the altar, jumping over pews, to transforming into Superman seems to be claimed as a true manifestation of the Spirit. It's no wonder that James Forbes in his 1989 work *The Holy Spirit and Preaching* coined the phrase "Spirit-shy Christians" to describe believers who find talking about the Spirit to be an intimidating and anxiety-filled experience. Preachers are not exempt, by the way. James Montgomery Boice, a well-respected pastor and Bible expositor, confessed his own neglect of the Spirit in his preaching: "I had been in the ministry for about seven years when my morning preaching through Philippians, the Sermon on the Mount, and John eventually brought me to the discourses of John 14–16, in which the work of the Holy Spirit is described. *Strange to say I had never* done any serious preaching on the Holy Spirit before that time"[3] (emphasis added).

As preachers we seem eager to tip our hats to the Holy Spirit's importance for our preaching, but we tend to clam up when asked to explain the Spirit's power in our own lives and in our own preaching. Once during my seminary days we had a chapel speaker who was going to discuss the life and preaching of Martyn Lloyd-Jones. I was excited because I knew Lloyd-Jones had some strong views about the Spirit and preaching. When the speaker finally came to Lloyd-Jones's views on the unction of the Holy Spirit for preaching, he said to us, "There are some beliefs that you are better off keeping to yourself and taking with you to the grave." With stifling statements like that, no wonder we have such a negative stigma about the Spirit!

Teaching Preaching

A third reason the Spirit is neglected in preaching today can be traced to the way we teach preaching in our colleges and seminaries. For starters, preaching typically ends up in the "practical" department rather than the "theological." As a result, students show up in preaching class and say with a sigh of relief, "Finally, something practical I can use in ministry." These pragmatically driven students eagerly but naively put behind all their "history, theology, and language stuff" so they can finally "let loose and just preach the Bible!"

As one who teaches preaching, I spend the first several weeks of my class laying down the theological foundation for preaching. One semester a student raised his hand and asked me, "When are we going to learn *how* to preach? This is all just a bunch of theory so far." Can I translate that: "This theological foundation is a waste of my time." With this type of mind-set, some students come to class wanting the "Top Ten Insights on How to Preach Like a Pro," "Seven Steps to Preaching with Success," "Five Days and Five Ways to Better Preaching," and "Three Secrets to Spirit-Filled Sermons."

---

3. James Montgomery Boice, "The Preacher and Scholarship," in *The Preacher and Preaching* (Phillipsburg, N.J.: Presbyterian and Reformed, 1986), 96.

Their expectations are nothing short of the miraculous: Teach me to preach with the passion of a Johnny Hunt, teach me to preach with the power of an Adrian Rogers, teach me to preach with the eloquence and imagination of a Jerry Vines, and teach me to preach with the theological depth of a John MacArthur. Disappointment sets in the minute I tell them that what they are seeing in the sermons of these preachers is the finished product that comes only at a great price: consistently walking with God in humility, daily seeking and surrendering to the Lord through prayer, and living clean and pure before God. Only after years of study, years of walking in holiness before God, and years of time spent alone with God in prayer is the chamber of the Spirit-filled heart ready to give birth to powerful preaching.

Preaching is not so much about you preparing a sermon to preach; preaching is about God preparing you—his vessel—to preach.

Let me challenge you to allow God to prepare you through kneeling in the power of his presence through unceasing prayer. Allow God to prepare you by soaking in the glory of his Word through diligent study of the Bible. Allow God to prepare your character through repentance, cleansing, and living above reproach before the Lord. Then you will find yourself walking into the pulpit as a transformed, Spirit-filled preacher who delivers a burden, not a sermon; who expresses convictions, not opinions; and who preaches to please God, not an audience.

We need to return to teaching the theological foundation of preaching from the classical theological doctrines of bibliology *and* pneumatology. Our students need to see the complementary relationship between Word and Spirit and to understand the proper function of sermon mechanics and sermon dynamics for preaching. They need to have as much zeal for the theological realities as they do for the how-to practicalities. Above all, they need to approach preaching with absolute dependence upon the Holy Spirit. The Spirit's role as the source and catalyst of all life-changing responses to preaching cannot be an afterthought; it is our consuming thought and prayer throughout our preparation and delivery!

This brief overview of the Spirit's absence should cause us to reexamine our own approach to preaching and ask ourselves some hard questions: How does the Holy Spirit inform my own theology of preaching? Have I thought through how the Word and the Spirit work together in preaching, or do I see them as theological opposites? How does my current sermon preparation demonstrate a dependence upon the Holy Spirit? What is my definition of preaching, and does it include the Spirit's ministries for preaching?

Ignorance, tradition, fear, and theological apathy can be overcome with a proper biblical theology of the Holy Spirit. Simply acknowledging the Spirit's presence is not enough. We must overcome our own Holy Spirit shyness and boldly invite the Spirit's gifts and ministries into the realm of our preaching. If preaching with power hinges on the Spirit's involvement, then it only makes sense to develop an approach to preaching that is Spirit dependent, Spirit led, and Spirit demonstrated.

I want to end this chapter by asking you to reflect on this statement: "If the Spirit of God is left out of preaching, preaching does not really happen." Would you say that more often than not in your own preaching, the Spirit has been left out? Perhaps after reading through this chapter, God is convicting you that you need to make a fresh surrender to his power in your life and in your preaching. Maybe you've quenched the Spirit instead of surrendering to the Spirit because of anger toward your church or toward your spouse or toward God. Perhaps unconfessed sin has hindered the Spirit's work in your life, and right now he's calling on you to turn from it and confess it. Can you honestly say the Spirit is in control of you right now—that you are filled and controlled by him? Ask God to give you a fresh dependence upon his Holy Spirit for your life, your preaching, and your church.

Chapter 2

What Is Spirit-Led Preaching?

And beginning with Moses and all the Prophets, he explained to them what was said in all the Scriptures concerning himself.

—*Luke 24:27*

As a small boy my youngest son loved trains. He could play for hours with his wooden Thomas the Train set, meticulously organizing the track into whatever configuration his mind could imagine. The train set taught him a few things. He learned that as long as he kept his hand on the train and kept the train on the track, it would move rather smoothly by the force of his hand. He also learned that if he took his hand off the train, or if the wheels on the train came off the track, the train slowed and eventually stopped.

Just as my son's hand powered the train down the tracks, we too need the gracious hand of God to empower our lives and our preaching. We must rely on the Spirit's propulsion to drive our sermons down the tracks established by the biblical text. I believe expository preaching is the best approach for keeping the sermonic train on the tracks of the biblical text. Look below at the illustration of the two sermonic trains. The first train represents one contemporary approach to expository preaching that highlights the text but neglects the Spirit. The second train represents the Spirit-led model that maintains that an equal emphasis on both Word and Spirit is critical for effective preaching.

In the first representative picture, the train (sermon) is driven by the text. In this model of expository preaching, the needs of the text are paramount: its grammatical structure, its interpretation, its explanation, and its application. The goal for such a view of expository preaching is typically correctly handling and properly presenting the biblical text. Success is often viewed in terms of how well the preacher's sermon points aligned with the text and whether the preacher kept the text in context. The Spirit's role is secondary to the text.

CURRENT MODEL IN EXPOSITORY PREACHING

Text-Driven Preaching: Text-driven preaching focuses on the presentation of the biblical text. The preacher's main concern is to address the needs of the text by explaining, illustrating, and applying the text. The text drives the sermon, and the Spirit's role is often Implicit.

The second picture represents a slightly different view of expository preaching, one in which the Spirit's role is more clarified. The key difference—and it is a crucial difference!—is that the sermon is driven along by the Holy Spirit in accordance with the biblical text. The needs of the text remain critical and paramount, but we understand that the Holy Spirit is the powerful engine of the sermonic train as it conforms to the biblical text revealed in Scripture. I imagine the Holy Spirit's power touching down on the tracks of the biblical text, and suddenly the combination of Word and Spirit together ignite into sermonic propulsion. The preacher's responsibility is not to push the train in his own strength; nor is it the preacher's responsibility to build new tracks to new places. The preacher's responsibility is to keep the train on the tracks! The biblical text becomes the train tracks that the Spirit-led preacher follows under the Spirit's illumination to the destination of Christological witness and Spirit-changed lives! The Word of God and the Spirit of God are both necessary, and both theological powerhouses must provide the fuel for our preaching.

PROPOSED MODEL OF SPIRIT-DRIVEN PREACHING

Spirit-Driven Preaching: Spirit-driven preaching is focused on the dynamic of the Spirit and the Spirit's text. The Spirit drives the sermon along the predetermined path of the biblical text. Spirit-driven preaching culminates in Christological witness and Spirit-filled living.

Spirit-led preaching thrives on the combustible power that ignites our preaching when the Spirit, the text, and the preacher all meet together in the sermon. Hence, Spirit-led preaching should be as narrow and as wide as the tracks of the biblical text. When we get off the tracks and go "rabbit chasing" in our sermons, then we can expect (and probably have experienced!) sluggishness in our preaching engine because our preaching has gotten off the Spirit-inspired track. If we don't get the sermon back on the tracks by returning to the heart of the biblical text, we will eventually come to a grinding and screeching halt because we are working against both the Word and the Spirit. On the ohter hand, when we find ourselves on the solid rails of the Spirit-inspired text, empowered by the Spirit's illuminating presence and driven by a passionate Christological motive to glorify Jesus, the train speeds along the tracks of the biblical text to its desired destination of spiritual transformation.

Defining Expository Preaching

Expository preaching in and of itself is no guarantee that the Holy Spirit will empower the preacher's message. Like any other kind of preaching, it can be mechanically flawless but completely lifeless if the Spirit does not empower it. The best definition of expository preaching will combine the theological catalyst of Word and Spirit working together through the preacher's Spirit-filled life, and this ultimately points to Jesus Christ and all his glory. It's time to emphasize the Spirit's role in preaching from the very beginning, by rightly defining and explicitly emphasizing the Spirit's key role in the homiletical process.

Some good definitions of expository preaching mention the Holy Spirit, but most do not capture the theological dynamic of Word and Spirit. Among modern definitions, one of the earliest references to the Holy Spirit comes from the work of Donald Miller in his 1957 book *The Way to Biblical Preaching*. He believes the biblical text is "made a living reality by the Holy Spirit" and that "the Spirit is the one who confronts the listener with the biblical truth."[1]

Haddon Robinson's classic definition emphasizes the Spirit's role in application, "which the Spirit first applies to the personality and experience of the preacher, then through him to his listeners."[2] Stephen and David Olford emphasize preaching as "Spirit-empowered explanation and proclamation."[3] Wayne McDill emphasizes the "enabling of the Holy Spirit,"[4] and Danny Akin

---

1. Donald G. Miller, *The Way to Biblical Preaching* (New York: Abingdon, 1957), 26.

2. Haddon W. Robinson, *Biblical Preaching: The Development and Delivery of Expository Messages* (Ada, Mich.: Baker Books, 1980), 20.

3. Stephen Olford and David Olford, *Anointed Expository Preaching* (Nashville: Broadman & Holman, 1998), 69.

4. Wayne McDill, *The Moment of Truth: A Guide to Effective Sermon Delivery* (Nashville: Broadman & Holman, 1999), 20.

emphasizes "expositional preaching that is done in submission to the Holy Spirit and the biblical revelation."[5]

For *Spirit-Led Preaching,* I have developed the following definition of expository preaching:

> Expository preaching is the Spirit-empowered proclamation of biblical truth derived from the illuminating guidance of the Holy Spirit by means of a verse-by-verse exposition of the Spirit-inspired text, with a view to applying the text by means of the convicting power of the Holy Spirit, first to the preacher's own heart, and then to the hearts of those who hear, culminating in an authentic and powerful witness to the living Word, Jesus Christ, and obedient, Spirit-filled living.

First and foremost, the Spirit's ministry for preaching is intentionally and explicitly identified in the following six ways: (1) the inspiration of the text, (2) the illumination of the preacher studying the text, (3) the conviction of the message, (4) the empowerment of the preacher, (5) the Spirit's Christological witness, and (6) Spirit-filled living. Second, the definition incorporates the theological categories of Word and Spirit by emphasizing the synergistic power that serves as the catalyst of Spirit-led preaching. Third, the definition is biblically sound and reflects the biblical theology of the Holy Spirit revealed in Scripture (John 16:13; 1 Cor. 2:4–13; Gal. 5:16, 22; 2 Tim. 3:16). Fourth, the definition's termination point is practical obedience in Spirit-filled living (transformative), as opposed to the exchange or transfer of biblical data (informative). Fifth, the definition properly emphasizes the Christological witness that the Spirit gives to the living Word by means of the written Word.

The underlying theological foundation of the Spirit-led definition assumes we are able to see the Holy Bible and the Holy Spirit as complementary to each other instead of competing against each other. Spirit-led preaching seeks to overcome the false dichotomy between the Word and the Spirit and instead unites them as the powerful catalyst for Spirit-demonstrated preaching. Rather than trying to balance

---

5. Daniel L. Akin, Ministry of Proclamation class notes, 2000, p. 13.

the Word with the Spirit, and the Spirit with the Word, I believe we need to return to the biblical understanding in which we are called to be completely filled and controlled by the Spirit (Eph. 5:18) and completely filled and controlled by the Word (Col. 3:16).

Why Expository Preaching?

Why is the Spirit-led model of preaching intentionally tied to expository preaching? Why not develop a Spirit-led approach to topical preaching, biographical preaching, or narrative preaching? First and foremost, as preachers we desire more than anything else for God to speak through our preaching. Yet in order for God to speak *through us,* we must first be convinced that God has already spoken *to us* in his Word (Heb. 1:1–4). Convinced of this, we make a commitment to preach Scripture because we know when we preach Scripture, people hear from God. How so? The Spirit of God takes the preached Word of God and pierces the human heart with conviction so that an unmistakable hearing from God takes place in the life of the listener. For the Spirit's witness to accompany our preaching, the revealed Word of God must be faithfully proclaimed. John 4:34 says, "For the one whom God has sent speaks the words of God, for God gives the Spirit without limit."

The prime reason for wedding the Holy Spirit to a ministry of exposition is that the same Holy Spirit who inspired the biblical text will minister through that same text when it is rightly divided and passionately proclaimed to our contemporary audience. The doctrine of inspiration demands exposition because God the Holy Spirit inscripturated his truth in words, phrases, sentences, and paragraphs. Therefore, a Spirit-led approach to preaching is naturally linked with the expository understanding of preaching because exposition at its core is testifying to what has been deposited already by the Holy Spirit in the Bible.

The strength of expository preaching, as opposed to other forms of preaching such as topical preaching, is that expository preaching respects not only the author's original intention but also the Holy Spirit's placement and sequencing of the text. Whereas topical preaching may freely pull verses out of context in order to establish the preacher's point (albeit a valid one), the careful expositor explains the text in its context and follows the sequence and the progression of the Spirit-deposited inspiration. How we handle the Spirit's inspiration is directly related to our view of the Bible. The higher our view of Scripture, the more careful we are to maintain authorial intent and to unpack the Spirit's work in its biblical context and framework.

The Benefits of Expository Preaching

The benefits of faithful exposition are numerous. First and foremost, expository preaching invokes the ministry of the Holy Spirit because the authority for the expository message comes from the text itself, the very Word of God. Hughes lists five clear benefits of expository preaching in general.

1. When you preach expositionally, you will preach texts that you would never voluntarily preach and would, perhaps, even purposely avoid.
2. When you preach expositionally, you never have to worry about what you are going to preach on Sunday.
3. When you preach expositionally, you will grow as a theologian because of systematic biblical exposition.
4. When you preach expositionally, you are always subject to the text. Exposition forces you to look to the Scripture for both your theme and structure.
5. When you preach expositionally, your authority is inherently derived from the text itself, not manufactured by the preacher.[6]

I would add a sixth benefit to Hughes's list. I believe expository preaching serves as the harness that holds the powerful combination of Word and Spirit together.

Above all, expository preaching assures us that we are keeping the sermonic train on the biblical tracks and helps us avoid unnecessary detours and breakdowns on our way to our final

6. R. Kent Hughes, "The Anatomy of Exposition: Logos, Ethos, and Pathos," *The Southern Baptist Journal of Theology* 3 (1999): 51.

destination of Spirit-filled living. Like my son's hand pushing along his toy train, I pray that the Holy Spirit will push us along the tracks of his inspired text until Jesus himself comes into focus and our audience submits to the Christological witness they see and respond like Thomas: "My Lord and my God!" (John 20:28).

Chapter 3

The Biblical Foundation for Spirit-Led Preaching: Paul, the Prophets, and Jesus

We who are ambassadors for God must not trifle, but we must tremble at God's Word. In addition, a preacher ought to know that he really possesses the Spirit of God, and that when he speaks there is an influence upon him that enables him to speak as God would have him, otherwise out of the pulpit he should go directly; he has no right to be there, he has not been called to preach God's truth.

—Spurgeon

The greatest sermon in the Bible was never written down and never made it into print. We know where it was preached—on the road to Emmaus. We know when it was preached—just days after the resurrection. We even know who preached it—Jesus! Call it a teaser if you will, but the biblical text gives us no more than this: "And beginning with Moses and all the Prophets, he explained to them what was said in all the Scriptures concerning himself" (Luke 24:27). You expect the next verse to read, "First, he went to Genesis and explained to them . . . then to Exodus, and he pointed out how he was . . ." Instead we are left to speculate and wonder. Yet one thing we can be sure of: Jesus himself preached himself from all the Scriptures.

I think Luke 24:27 is a great description of the expository preacher's task: to explain to our audience what is said in all the Scriptures about Jesus. This does not simply limit us to the Gospels, which lend themselves readily to testify about Christ and his life and ministry. Remember, the Scriptures Christ was referring to in Luke 24:27 didn't include the New Testament because it had not yet been written. We preachers must practice in our pulpits what we believe in our theology: Christ is the grand theme, the singular message, and the supreme subject of *all* the Bible. Whereas the Old Testament predicts Christ, the New Testament presents Christ. Both Testaments bear Christological witness. If Jesus used the Old Testament to preach about himself, then so should we!

I would like to add a theological twist to the plot at this point. Many scholars, including Sidney Greidanus, rightly say that Jesus Christ is the common denominator of both the Old and New Testaments. What you typically don't hear scholars say is that *the Holy Spirit* serves as a common denominator between the Old and New Testaments. In other words the Spirit's inspiration of the Bible applies to both the Old and New Testaments—total, verbal inspiration. Consequently the Spirit's witness to Christ is not limited to the New Testament alone; Christological witness is present in the Old Testament precisely because the Spirit of God is present in both Testaments.

This chapter demonstrates that Spirit-led preaching has its biblical foundation in both the prophets of the Old Testament and Paul's preaching in the New Testament. We will find that the Holy Spirit's empowerment (anointing) serves as the common denominator of proclamation in both Testaments, solidly grounding Spirit-led preaching in the biblical witness.

The Prophets

When Jesus stood in the synagogue at the inauguration of his public ministry in Nazareth and read from the Isaiah scroll, he was purposely aligning himself with the rich preaching tradition of the Old Testament prophets. The Bible says of Jesus in Luke 4:18–19, "The scroll of the prophet Isaiah was handed to him. Unrolling it, he found the place where it is written: 'The Spirit of the Lord is on me, because he has anointed me to preach good news to the poor. He has sent me to proclaim freedom for the prisoners and recovery of sight for the blind, to release the oppressed, to proclaim the year of the Lord's favor.'" It is worth noting that before Jesus began his public preaching ministry, the Bible says in Luke 4:1 that he was "full of the Holy Spirit" and also that he was "led by the Spirit."

Simply put, our Lord's communion with the Holy Spirit was established *before* he took on his public ministry of teaching and preaching. In fact, a divine prerogative is revealed in Isaiah 61:1–2 and embodied in Christ's own preaching ministry. First, the Spirit of the Lord came upon him, a sign of empowerment and authority established by the Old Testament prophetic tradition in figures like Elijah and Elisha. Second, the task of ministry (preaching/ proclamation) was carried out under the empowerment of the Spirit. Consequently, the prerequisite to powerful proclamation is the active presence of the Holy Spirit in your life. The Spirit's empowerment was evident before Jesus even opened his mouth to preach. So may it be with us today!

It is also important to note that the Spirit's empowerment or anointing came in direct relationship to the scroll (the Word of God) being handed to Jesus. The implication is compelling support for Spirit-led expository preaching: even the living Word used the written Word under the anointing of the Holy Spirit as an authentication of the authority and power of his preaching. Jesus referred to the complementary relationship between his words and the Spirit when he said, "The Spirit gives life; the flesh counts for nothing. The words I have spoken to you are spirit and they are life" (John 6:63). Note how the theological themes of Word ("the words I have spoken") and Spirit ("the Spirit gives life") combine to present the life-giving word that has transformative power.

In John 6:63, the Greek word for "Spirit" and "spirit" is the same in the Greek text (*pneuma*), giving the implication that the Holy Spirit speaking through Jesus produced "spirit" words that when appropriated by faith give everlasting life. The idea is not that the words have the *potential* to bring life but that the words themselves *are* life. When I preach Scripture, I am preaching the Spirit's words, and the Spirit's words; not my words, bring life to sinners who are dead in their trespasses and sins.

Jesus stood firmly in the historic heritage of prophetic preaching as the ultimate fulfillment and incarnation of all that the prophets in the Old Testament stood for as the mouthpieces of God. The Old Testament is replete with examples of the Spirit empowering God's prophets for proclamation. Numbers 11:25 mentions that the Spirit "rested" on the seventy elders and they "prophesied." In Numbers 24:2–3, the Spirit of God "came upon" Balaam, and he "uttered his oracle." When Samuel anointed Saul as king over Israel, he told Saul in 1 Samuel 10:6, "The Spirit of the LORD will come upon you in power, and you will prophesy with them; and you will be changed into a different person." The prophet Micah said, "But as for me, I am filled with power, with the Spirit of the LORD, and with justice and might, to declare to Jacob his transgression, to Israel his sin" (Mic. 3:8).

Notice the pattern of the filling "with power, with the Spirit of the LORD" preceding the action "to declare." Preachers must decide early in their preaching ministries that they have to be continually filled with the Spirit of God before they can powerfully preach the Word of God. Anointed lives give birth to anointed preaching.

Furthermore, God's empowerment of his prophets and kings demonstrates that they in and of themselves were not able to carry out their God-given tasks apart from divine enablement. Deuteronomy 18:18 establishes the office of the prophet (*nabhi*) as one in which God imparts the message to the messenger: "I will put my words in his mouth, and he will tell them everything I command him." The role of the prophet is clearly one of spokesperson or reporter. The *nabhi* is literally one who speaks forth a message. Hence the message is always preceded by a sense of divine enablement or the Spirit's empowering presence, often referred to as "anointing."

In the Old Testament the Spirit's presence was not an indwelling, permanent presence as in the New Testament, but rather the Spirit was given at specific times for specific tasks and for temporary periods of time. In the New Testament the indwelling Spirit is universal for all believers whereas in the Old Testament the Spirit's presence or anointing was given to selected individuals. Despite the distinction between Testaments, the pattern of the Spirit's empowerment before public proclamation serves as a strong biblical argument for adopting a Spirit-led approach to expository preaching.

Paul's Theology of Preaching

Moving from the Old Testament to the New Testament, Paul's homiletic found in 1 Corinthians 2 and other passages will serve as further biblical evidence for Spirit-led preaching. First, Paul believed that the power in preaching must come from the Holy Spirit, not human manipulation or "human wisdom, lest the cross of Christ be emptied of its power" (1 Cor. 1:17; cf. 2:4). Second, Paul believed preaching must center on the person and work of Jesus Christ, with a specific emphasis on the cross as the basis for everything Christian. Paul said, "We preach Christ crucified . . . the power . . . and . . . wisdom of God" (1 Cor. 1:23–24). Third, Paul's preaching was driven by his doctrine of inspiration found in 2 Timothy 3:16 as well as 1 Corinthians 2:12–14. As a result, Paul believed in the profitability of all Scripture and consequently preached the whole counsel of God (Acts 20:27).

Paul's Preaching: Spirit Empowered

Paul believed in the power of the gospel and the power of the Spirit. He declared in Romans 1:16 that the gospel is the power of God unto salvation. He stated in 1 Corinthians 2:4 that his preaching was powerfully Spirit demonstrated. Paul was not afraid of the Word or the Spirit. Paul's descriptive statement to the Thessalonians reveals his Spirit-led understanding of preaching; he declared the gospel came not simply with words but "with power, with the Holy Spirit and with deep conviction" (1 Thess. 1:5).

Rejection of Human Manipulation. A Spirit-empowered theology of preaching begins with the rejection of all human means of manipulation and persuasion. It totally depends on God as the supernatural source of power that changes and transforms lives through the Word and the Spirit. Paul clearly wanted to distinguish himself from the rhetoricians of his day who had improper motives and used questionable means in their philosophic and oratorical presentations. Paul told the Corinthian church that he was not in it for the money. Instead, he bore the authority of one sent from God: "Unlike so many, we do not peddle the word of God for profit. On the contrary, in Christ we speak before God with sincerity, like men sent from God" (2 Cor. 2:17). Paul distanced himself from the underhanded and shady techniques used by the professional rhetoricians and built his preaching ministry on the Holy Spirit and God's power.

The most direct statement of the apostle Paul's rejection of human means in the preaching of the gospel comes from 1 Corinthians 2:1–5:

> When I came to you, brothers, I did not come with eloquence or superior wisdom as I proclaimed to you the testimony about God. For I resolved to know nothing while I was with you except Jesus Christ and him crucified. I came to you in weakness and fear, and with much trembling. My message and my preaching were not with wise and persuasive words, but with a demonstration of the Spirit's power, so that your faith might not rest on men's wisdom, but on God's power.

First, Paul clearly rejected eloquence, superior wisdom, and persuasive wording. "Eloquence" refers to a speaker's oratorical skills. "Wisdom" (*sophia*) pertains in this context to philosophical argument. Paul's rejection of flowery oratory and manipulative argumentation was based on his theological understanding of salvation as a grace given by God, not an argument won by man. Paul's preaching of the gospel was not accomplished by human wisdom under any false pretense because his gospel was revealed from heaven "so that your faith might not rest on men's wisdom, but on God's power."

Someone once said, "If I can talk you into your salvation, there is a good chance somebody else can talk you out of it." As preachers today we need to avoid using human pressure and manipulative gimmicks in the pulpit as tools of persuasion. Instead we should trust the Spirit to bring about his conviction. Human-induced guilt will quickly fade away after the message is over, but the Spirit's conviction sticks to the heart long after you have finished preaching.

You may be able to change a person's mind for the moment, but only the Spirit of God can change his heart for all eternity.

Paul's doctrine of salvation as a work of the Spirit through the proclamation of the Word drove his biblical theology of preaching. Paul declared in Romans 10 that you cannot call on the Lord and be saved until you hear the gospel (Word), and you cannot hear the gospel unless someone preaches it to you. Then he said in 1 Corinthians 12:3 that "no one can say, 'Jesus is Lord,' except by the Holy Spirit." So which is it? Is it the preached Word, or is it the Holy Spirit? It's both! Paul's preaching was Spirit led and gospel centered because he knew that was the only combination that could save souls. Paul's Spirit-dependent and Christ-centered approach to preaching models for us the synergistic power of the Word and Spirit together.

This is not to say that Paul did not use persuasive argument, especially when reasoning or proving Christ from the Scriptures. His ministry in Athens began in the synagogue with Paul reasoning: "So he reasoned [to think through] in the synagogue with the Jews and the God-fearing Greeks, as well as in the marketplace day by day with those who happened to be there" (Acts 17:17). Yet when he delivered his Mars Hill sermon, he proclaimed, "Now what you worship as something unknown I am going to proclaim to you" (Acts 17:23). Paul proved that proclamation does not preclude logic, reasoning, or argument. His passionate gospel proclamation was only complemented by his reasoning from the Scriptures.

Acts 28:23 finds Paul before Festus where "from morning till evening he explained and declared to them the kingdom of God and tried to convince them about Jesus from the Law of Moses and from the Prophets." Notice the combination: the explanation and declaration of Jesus from the Bible, all carried out in the Spirit's power.

The Preacher as Herald. In Paul's theology of preaching, is the preacher primarily a teacher, a philosopher, a negotiator, a rhetorician, a communicator, or something altogether different? What does Paul identify as the preacher's primary task? Paul's understanding of the role of the preacher takes shape from 1 Corinthians 2 as well. Paul's word for preaching in 1 Corinthians

2 is *kerygma,* which means "proclamation" or "announcement." In 2 Timothy 4:2, Paul charged Timothy to "preach (*kērussō*) the Word." The word Paul used for preaching comes from the *kērux* family of words which have a root meaning of "the man who is commissioned by his ruler or the state to call out with a clear voice some item of news and so to make it known." The word pictures the preacher as a herald, whose sole duty is to "announce, make known, and proclaim aloud." Paul's biblical theology of preaching is grounded in the clear understanding of biblically defined roles— first, the preacher's role is to proclaim and announce the message from God's Word; and second, the Spirit's role is to bear witness that the proclamation is indeed the Word of God by causing its truthfulness to resonate within the hearts of listeners. The Spirit gives affirmation to the preacher's proclamation.

Demonstration of the Spirit. Paul stated that his preaching was "a demonstration of the Spirit's power." The Greek word for demonstration *(apodeixis)* occurs only in 1 Corinthians 2:4 and carries the idea of providing proof. In Paul's theology of preaching, the Holy Spirit's unseen dynamic at work in the preacher and the hearers is the "proof" or confirmation that God's Word is powerful, active, and living. Just as the Spirit testifies to our salvation (Rom. 8:16), the Spirit also testifies or "proves" to our listeners that we are preaching the Word of God and that they are hearing the Word of God. The Holy Spirit is the divine communicator. He inspires the Word, illumines the Word, and authenticates the Word.

Jesus taught his disciples about the "proofing" or "confirming" ministry of the Holy Spirit when he said in John 16:13, "But when he, the Spirit of truth, comes, he will guide you into all truth." Hence, Paul's preaching is powerful because it carries the divine confirmation, the divine "proof," given by means of the Holy Spirit's inward authentication. The Spirit's authentication is the inward burning conviction produced by the Spirit that affirms what is being said is indeed true and demands obedience. When preachers and teachers refer to the Holy Spirit as the sacred communicator, they are referring to the Holy Spirit placing his seal of approval on the message being preached. Powerful preaching happens when the audience hears the preacher's audible voice proclaiming the Word as the Spirit's internal voice authenticates the Word so that people leave asking, "Were not our hearts burning within us while he . . . opened the Scriptures to us?" (Luke 24:32).

How do we activate the Spirit's authenticating ministry for preaching? My conviction is that the closer we align ourselves with the Spirit-inspired text (exposit what is already placed in the text by the Spirit), the greater the Spirit's authentication will be in the hearts of those who hear us. Through prayer we ask for the Spirit to empower us and to confirm the truthfulness and authority of our message in the hearts of those to whom we preach. We pray for Spirit-opened ears and Spirit-softened hearts. I find this general principle to be true: the Spirit affirms what the preacher first confirms in the Word of God.

Sin: The Need for the Spirit's Empowerment. We need the Holy Spirit because of one simple reason: sin. Sinful human beings need a sense of conviction, of supernatural verification, and internal confirmation because sin has darkened our hearts and minds. Since the goal of all preaching is the glory of God by means of spiritual transformation, preaching is not like every other form of communication where the goal is to get an idea across or to transfer information from source to receptor. Paul's biblical theology of preaching finds its foundation in the theological doctrines of anthropology and sin. In Romans 3:23 Paul summarized, "For all have sinned and fall short of the glory of God." As a consequence of sin, Paul remarked in Romans 3:11 that there is "no one who understands, no one who seeks God."

Jesus pointed out the challenge original sin presents for preaching when he said, "For this people's heart has become calloused; they hardly hear with their ears, and they have closed their eyes" (Matt. 13:15). Paul's conviction regarding the sinfulness and total depravity of all human beings necessitates the involvement of supernatural power in his preaching.

In its purest form, preaching is literally an attempt to raise the dead to spiritual life in Christ. Since spiritual corpses do not hear very well, something else must quicken them to the truth of the living God. The supernatural must break in on them so that they recognize and submit to the voice of the living God speaking his word to their hearts by the quickening of the Spirit of God. The depravity of man necessitates Spirit-empowered preaching because only the Holy Spirit can bring the spiritually dead to life in supernatural, resurrection fashion. If we are convinced this is true, then it only makes sense to approach preaching with a Spirit-dependent attitude and a Spirit-led mind-set so that we foster the atmosphere in which the Spirit can move and work.

Go back with me once again to Luke 24 and the disciples on the Emmaus road. Jesus, in a post-resurrection appearance, revealed himself to the disciples on the road to Emmaus. The preaching of Jesus resulted in the disciples' introspection: "Were not our hearts burning within us while he talked with us on the road and opened the Scriptures to us?" (Luke 24:32). Every preacher longs for his listener's hearts to be set on fire by what he is saying, yet the preacher cannot forget the preceding verse: "Then their eyes were opened and they recognized him." The opening of the eyes came before the burning of the heart. What kind of preaching opens the eyes of listeners? The kind that always "recognizes" Jesus! The Spirit opens the eyes, but the man of God must take the Word of God and present a clear picture of Jesus. Not only must you paint them a clear picture of Jesus, but you, as God's preacher, must incarnate the truth you are preaching about the Savior as well.

> Every time you preach, picture someone in the congregation making this request: "Sir, we would like to see Jesus."
> —John 12:21

The passion of preaching Christ should emanate from our total being, demonstrating that we are experiencing the Spirit's work in our own hearts as we preach. We must spend more time pleading with God to open the eyes of our listeners and less time worrying about remembering our illustrations, our punch lines, or our transition statements.

The Spirit and Weakness. We need to ask ourselves, "Is there a certain environment or attitude in which the Spirit's empowering ministry seems to flourish?" First Corinthians 2:3 suggests that the Spirit's empowerment often takes place in the context of human weakness and frailty: "I came to you in weakness and fear, and with much trembling." Why human weakness and frailty? I believe Paul physically manifested the gravity and magnitude of the task to which God had called him. In our weakness and the confession of our own human frailty, we fall surrendered before a holy, all-powerful God and plead for his divine intervention to help us stand and open our mouths and preach from our hearts. Weakness creates dependency, dependency fosters humility, and humility gives birth to empowerment: "Humble yourselves before the Lord, and he will lift you up" (James 4:10) and "My grace is sufficient for you, for my power is made perfect in weakness" (2 Cor. 12:9).

Paul's Preaching: Christ Centered

A second feature of Paul's approach to preaching is his strong emphasis on the Christ-centered gospel. If the Spirit's empowerment is the *dynamic* of Paul's preaching, then the gospel of Jesus Christ serves as the *content* of Paul's preaching. Paul's approach to determining his subject matter for preaching was refreshingly simple: "For I resolved to know nothing while I was with you except Jesus Christ and him crucified" (1 Cor. 2:2). He told the Corinthians, "For we do not preach ourselves, but Jesus Christ as Lord, and ourselves as your servants for Jesus' sake" (2 Cor. 4:5). In Ephesians 3:8, Paul stated that he was commissioned by the grace of God to "preach to the Gentiles the unsearchable riches of Christ." Undoubtedly, the heart and soul of Paul's preaching was the gospel of Jesus Christ.

Paul located the power of his preaching ministry in the cross of Jesus: "For Christ did not send me to baptize, but to preach the gospel—not with words of human wisdom, lest the cross of Christ be emptied of its power" (1 Cor. 1:17). He told the Corinthians, "But we preach Christ crucified: a stumbling block to Jews and foolishness to Gentiles, but to those whom God has called, both Jews and Greeks, *Christ the power of God* and the wisdom of God" (1 Cor. 1:23–24, emphasis added). For Paul, Christian preaching is centered on the cross because the cross is the fulfillment of the redemptive message of the Bible. Christocentric messages focus on the redemptive gospel of

Jesus Christ and carry with them the singular purpose of proclaiming Christ crucified and resurrected as the answer for humanity's sin.

> The key question every preacher must ask is: How am I going to put Christ at the heart and center of this message in such a compelling manner that all who hear will either reject him in unbelief or embrace him as Lord?

The need to preach the cross of Jesus Christ has not changed since Paul's day. One Easter season on Palm Sunday I was preaching on Luke 9:23: "If anyone would come after me, he must deny himself and take up his cross daily and follow me." Nearing the end of the message, I slowly walked over to the large wooden cross that our choir and drama team had used earlier in the service for their musical. As I took off my jacket, I raised the cross out of its wooden holder and struggled just to get it on my back in a carrying position (quite honestly, I had not rehearsed carrying the cross, and its bulkiness caught me off guard; I did so only out of prompting by the Spirit and a desire to visually drive home the message). As I stumbled with the cross on my back to the center of the stage, I concluded the message with the cross still on my back, breathing heavily from its weight and the struggle to bear it. Never before in my own preaching ministry had the meaning of what it meant to take up the cross been so powerfully and visually demonstrated.

Yet the real lesson for me came on Monday morning while I was having my quiet time with the Lord. A slight irritation was coming from the palms of my hands, and when I looked I saw splinters just underneath the top layer of my skin. At first I was dumbfounded as to where they came from; then it dawned on me that they were from the day before when I had picked up the cross. As I started to dig them out of my skin, the Holy Spirit impressed on my heart that those splinters were there as a powerful reminder of what preaching the cross of Christ is all about. We must preach the cross of Christ with such conviction, power, compulsion, and passion that when we wake up on Monday we can still feel the splinters of the old rugged cross in the palms of our hands.

Paul's Preaching: Word Based

In addition to being Spirit empowered and Christ centered, Paul's approach to preaching uses God's Word as the medium through which the Holy Spirit operates. Paul said in 1 Corinthians 2:13, "This is what we speak, not in words taught us by human wisdom *but in words taught by the Spirit,* expressing spiritual truths in spiritual words" (emphasis added). Paul's preaching centered upon the revelation of God, aided by the Spirit's understanding (1 Cor. 2:12). Spirit-empowered preaching is the result of proclaiming the Spirit-taught word that gives a Christ-centered witness and calls for a Spirit-filled response. Consequently, the Holy Spirit not only empowers the message; he provides the source and substance of the message in the Scripture that he has inspired.

This is why we must preach the Bible. We have not received revelation in the way the apostle Paul received it, but we have received what Paul recorded in Scripture. The bottom line for preaching is this: when the Bible is expounded, God speaks. When the Bible is heard, the voice of God is heard. God speaks by his Spirit, through his Word, using our voice to echo what is already in the Scriptures.

Conclusion

Both the prophets of the Old Testament and Paul in the New Testament serve as convincing evidence that the proclamation of God's Word is first and foremost a spiritual dynamic that cannot be accomplished apart from divine empowerment. Like Paul, we must establish our preaching on the theological dynamics of the Spirit and the Word witnessing together in Christological harmony. A robust theology of preaching, grounded in Word and Spirit, gives us the biblical foundation for Spirit-led preaching.

Chapter 4

Recovering the Doctrine of Illumination for Spirit-Led Preaching

*Therefore, as we can never come to Christ, unless
we are drawn by the Spirit of God, so when we are
drawn, we are raised both in mind and in heart above
the reach of our own understanding. For illuminated
by him, the soul receives, as it were, new eyes for the
contemplation of heavenly mysteries, by the splendor
of which it was never before dazzled. And thus the
human intellect, irradiated by the light of the Holy
Spirit, then begins to relish those things which pertain
to the kingdom of God, for which before it had not the
smallest taste.*

—*John Calvin*

Imagine a Tuesday night home Bible study where members of the group are asked to read and prepare questions on John 2. After class members arrive and have their refreshments, the Bible study begins. As typical of the study, each member is asked a simple question by the group leader: "How did God speak to you this week?" As they are going around the circle sharing their insights, a controversy erupts over whether John 2—the wedding feast at Cana—was proof that Jesus supported social drinking. Mike, a new Christian, believes the fact that Jesus turned the water into wine is evidence that God condones the use of alcohol, at least in moderation and during times of celebration. Bill, the group leader, tries to steer the conversation away from alcohol and back toward authorial intent by focusing the group on the intended meaning of John's Gospel: "But these are written that you may believe that Jesus is the Christ, the Son of God, and that by believing you may have life in his name" (John 20:31).

Mike, however, cannot believe that his understanding and insights into John 2 could be wrong. After all, he had just read a few weeks earlier in the same Gospel of John that the Holy Spirit would tell him the truth: "But when he, the Spirit of truth, comes, he will guide you into all truth" (John 16:13). The longer Bill tries to reason with Mike, the more perplexed Mike becomes. Finally, out of pure frustration, Mike declares, "This is my interpretation and the Spirit gave it to me."

How do we respond to Mike's statement? How do we keep a Bible study from spiraling into a series of opinions that everyone claims are "God given"? Does the same Holy Spirit give different interpretations to different people—even from the same biblical text?

The Spirit in Hermeneutics

One difficulty of studying the illumination of the Spirit is that it defies objective or empirical study. No amount of verifiable evidence or objective testing can "prove" that the Spirit's illumination has taken place in the heart and mind of the biblical interpreter. The Spirit's work of illumination is intuitive and individual, which is why we can read the Bible and hear the Bible preached and have this compelling conviction that God is speaking directly to us and to our specific life situation.

Though the Spirit's work in our hearts is subjective and unique to each individual believer, that subjective aspect must always be governed by the grammatical-historical method of biblical interpretation that is anchored in authorial intent. Interpretations of the Bible that make no reference to authorial intent almost always end up misreading the text because the Holy Spirit inspired the biblical text following certain predictable rules and guidelines that we can identify: language, grammar, genre, and so forth. Therefore, it would not make sense for the Spirit to contradict his work of inspiration by providing "new" illumination that goes against or contradicts what he said in his inspired Word.

The Spirit is God, and for the Spirit to illumine the biblical text in a way that does not honor his inspiration would be a contradiction of his divine nature. Consequently, we do not disregard the role of the reader of the biblical text, but instead we assert that the reader should always be subject to the author's original intent. So a reader of the biblical text who puts the Spirit's illumination at odds with the Spirit-intended meaning of the text is actually dishonoring the Spirit's original work in inspiration.

Inspiration

The establishment and acceptance of the biblical text as the true Word of God is fundamental to starting the hermeneutical process. If we are not convinced the text is inspired by the Spirit and therefore trustworthy (1 Cor. 2:11; 2 Tim. 3:16), then we can rest assured we will not receive the illumination offered by the same Holy Spirit who inspired the text to begin with. Inspiration and illumination are part of the total package of God's revelation to us and must be embraced as a powerful combination. When you begin to question the accuracy and authority of Scripture, you are not offending the ancient historical writers; you are offending the living Holy Spirit who inspired it.

Inspiration is the biblical doctrine that affirms the superintending work of the Holy Spirit over the human authors of Scripture so that what we have recorded in Scripture is the Word of God. The Spirit's oversight of the process of inscripturation guarantees that the canon of sixty-six books we call the Bible is completely true and without error. The Spirit safeguarded the process but also allowed for the human authors to express themselves in the thought forms and culture of their day. The doctrine of inspiration causes us to approach Scripture with a sense of reverence and awe, for we know what we have in the Bible is God's revelation to man. His means of inspiration—the Holy Spirit—now lives in us as believers as a guide to that revelation. We honor the Spirit's inspiration when we confess the truthfulness of his Scriptures through prayer before we enter into our times of study. We honor the Spirit when we recognize God's holy, authoritative, true, and altogether wonderful Word (Ps. 119).

The Spirit's inspiration also establishes the authority of the Bible for us so that we as preachers do not stand over the Bible in judgment but under the Bible in submission. We approach the Word of God with an attitude of holiness and brokenness before we even begin to study it. Who are we to look into the Word of God and to know things that even the angels long to look into? As believers we approach Scripture differently than we would a newspaper or a Web page. We read a newspaper or Web page for information, but we read the Word of God for transformation.

Differences between Inspiration and Illumination

Both inspiration and illumination are ministries of the same Holy Spirit, but this common source does not mean the terms are interchangeable. The key difference between the doctrine of inspiration and the doctrine of illumination is this: inspiration is a *completed* process that guaranteed the truthfulness of the Bible by the Spirit's superintending of the revelation we have recorded in Scripture, whereas illumination is a *continuing* work of the Spirit that guides us into all truth (John 16:13). This means that the Spirit's illumination is the guide to his inspiration, and we desperately need his guidance into truth because we are sinful, fallen, and fallible human beings.

This is precisely why the Spirit's illumination can never be said to result in "infallibility." Revelation alone is infallible; illumination is not. That's the safeguard for Spirit-led preaching. Whatever the Spirit illumines in our hearts should emanate from objective revelation, not mystical visions that take us outside the revelation God has given us in his Word.

Does God Speak?

This understanding of illumination begs the question: does God still speak to us today? My answer to this question is grounded in the Holy Spirit's illumination. Yes, God speaks today because he speaks to me by his Spirit through his Word. Is the Spirit giving me new teaching that is higher and superior to Scripture? No, the Spirit is illuminating what is already recorded in God's Word, so that the Word of God is quickened to my heart for every need of my life.

Much of the tension between charismatics and evangelicals can be traced to a misunderstanding of the doctrine of illumination. Charismatics charge that evangelicals hold to completed revelation and a closed canon; therefore, God does not speak to us today because he has definitively and finally spoken to us in the revelation of Christ (Heb. 1:1–4). On the other hand, evangelicals charge that charismatics try to supersede the Scriptures by seeking a "fresh word of knowledge" all the time instead of honoring the Word already given in Scripture.

As an evangelical Christian, I believe God has spoken to believers definitively and sufficiently in his Word. Hebrews 1:1–2 says, "In the past God spoke to our forefathers through the prophets at many times and in various ways, but in these last days he has spoken to us by his Son, whom he appointed heir of all things, and through whom he made the universe." The verb translated "has spoken" speaks of a past-completed action with continuing or abiding effect. To say we need a new word of knowledge today as believers undermines the sufficiency and completeness of the Word of God. We cannot improve on the Father's revelation of his Son recorded in Scripture because it is sufficient for our salvation and our lives.

The completeness of revelation does not mean that God does not speak and interact with us as his children. In one sense all believers have to agree that God speaks to them, for how else would we know what we need to repent of. How else would we know what priorities we need to change? How else would we know what promises we need for the day? How else would we receive the encouragement we need to stand strong in our faith? This is what makes our faith living and active, much as the Word of God is described as living and active in Hebrews 4:12. So the Spirit of God through the Word of God speaks purposely to our hearts so that we truly believe we have heard a timely and applicable word from the Lord.

Now the big question is this: *How* does God speak to day about these very things? I believe the answer is, by I... illumination through his inspired Word. The Spirit of God within me applies the Word of God to my heart in a fresh and powerful way every day. This is why we desperately need to recover the Spirit's illumination for preaching. This is the reason we cannot preach someone else's sermon. We can learn from another's sermon, but we cannot preach it word for word because we bypass the Spirit's illumination in our own hearts and lives. You cannot borrow someone else's illumination. Trying to reheat someone else's sermon and serve it up as yours is like trying to microwave a frozen dinner—warm in some spots, frozen in others—but worst of all, you are still hungry after you eat it!

Defining Illumination

Before we go any further, let's nail down exactly what we mean when we say "illumination." Spirit-led preaching will adopt the following vocabulary for the Spirit's illumination, based on the work of New Testament scholar Bob Stein:

- *Meaning.* The meaning of a text is that pattern of meaning the author willed to convey by the words (shareable symbols) he used.
- *Implications.* Implications are those meanings in a text of which the author was unaware but nevertheless legitimately fall within the pattern of meaning he willed.
- *Significance.* Significance refers to how a reader responds to the meaning of the text. It involves the reader's will and is the choice to say yes or no to the call of the text for obedient living.[1]

Using Stein's clearly defined terms, let me share with you my definition:

Illumination is the process whereby the Holy Spirit
so impresses, convinces, and convicts the believer as to
the truthfulness and significance of the author's intended

---

1. Robert Stein, *A Basic Guide to Interpreting the Bible* (Grand Rapids: Baker Books, 1994), 43.

meaning in the text that a change in action, attitude, or belief occurs, resulting in a more transformed, Spirit-filled life.

First, the above definition is biblically sound. The definition includes "truthfulness" because the Scripture says in John 16:13, "But when he, the Spirit of truth, comes, he will guide you into all truth. He will not speak on his own; he will speak only what he hears, and he will tell you what is yet to come." The Holy Spirit's role is to lead us to passionately embrace and faithfully obey the truth of God's Word so that the Spirit's transforming and sanctifying work continually refines us into the likeness of Christ. The Spirit's illumination tailors God's Word to our own hearts by identifying where and how to appropriate God's Word into our own specific situations.

Second, the definition includes the phrase "impresses, convinces, and convicts" because the Bible says in John 16:8–11 that this is precisely the Spirit's ministry to us as believers. The word *convict* means that the Holy Spirit makes God's Word stick. It sticks in your mind, it sticks in your conscience, and it sticks in your heart. The Spirit as Counselor is pinning his inspired truth to our illuminated hearts. He drives the truth deep inside us and desires our glad submission and yieldedness to his illuminating work.

Third, the definition also includes the word *change,* indicating the dynamic process whereby the application of the biblical truth by the Holy Spirit impacts us holistically. Hence, a Spirit-inspired text studied by a Spirit-indwelled preacher coupled with a Spirit-illumined heart will inevitably result in Spirit-led preaching that calls people to Spirit-filled living which ultimately glorifies God. "This is to my Father's glory, that you bear much fruit, showing yourselves to be my disciples" (John 15:8).

The 1 Corinthians 2:14 Debate: Can an Unbeliever Understand the Bible?

One of the controversies concerning the role of the Holy Spirit's illumination in the interpretive process ironically comes from how we interpret a disputed passage to begin with. In 1 Corinthians 2:14, Paul wrote, "The man without the Spirit does not accept the things that come from the Spirit of God, for they are foolishness to him, and he cannot understand them, because they are spiritually discerned." The debate over this passage centers on two main thoughts: (1) whether the Spirit's role in interpretation is to give believers cognitive understanding of the actual intended meaning of the author, which is unavailable to the unbeliever; or (2) whether the Spirit's role is to bring about the conviction of the truthfulness, authority, and significance of the Scripture for the believer, which is unavailable to the unbeliever.

In other words, does the phrase "cannot understand them" imply cognitive knowledge of the mind or knowledge by personal experience? Do unbelievers actually understand what the text is saying but then reject it as "foolishness"? Or does the meaning of the text somehow elude unbelievers, leading them to reject the entire enterprise as "foolishness"?

The Spirit Teaches Meaning

The first school of thought in the debate on the meaning of 1 Corinthians 2:14 is found in the writings of A. W. Pink, Abraham Kuyper, John Calvin, Hanley Moule, and C. H. MacKintosh, to name a few. This school of thought believes that only through the illumination of the Holy Spirit can a text's *meaning* be understood. Therefore, only believers who by definition have the Spirit can understand the text. As a result, this school of thought asserts that there are actually two sets of logic at work in the world: one for believers, given and aided by the Spirit, and one for unbelievers, unaided by the Spirit and left to their own futile thinking. The Spirit gives the cognitive comprehension of the text to the interpreter, so he knows what the passage means. In this view the Holy Spirit is seen as the necessary instrument for comprehending the meaning of the text, and no understanding of meaning (mental or experiential) comes to the believer apart from the Spirit.

The Spirit Teaches Significance

The problem with the "Spirit Teaches Meaning" position is that it does not sufficiently explain what is going on in 1 Corinthians 2:14. The verse can be wrongly interpreted to say that only Christians can understand the meaning of the Bible because they alone receive special assistance from the Spirit when they read it. Yet a closer look at the passage reveals that the Greek word for "understands" carries the connotation of understanding something by experience, not cognition or "mind-only" understanding. If Paul wanted to communicate the idea of an intellectual assent to facts, he could have used the Greek word *oida,* but he did not.

Paul does not deny that unbelievers can grasp the *meaning* of the text through normal means of study that are available to all who are willing to learn the vocabulary and grammar of the Bible. A present-tense participle is a present-tense participle, whether the reader is a Christian or not. I think Paul is saying that once unbelievers understand what the text says, they reject it because in their unregenerate judgment it is "foolishness" or nonsense to their unredeemed minds. First Corinthians 1:18 substantiates this position because Paul says the message of the cross is "foolishness to those who are perishing," that is, to those who are still in their natural, unredeemed minds and without the aid of the Spirit's illumination.

We do not deny that people without the Spirit can know basic Bible facts—names, dates, places, and even themes and main ideas of the biblical revelation. But what they do not have is a vital relationship with the Holy Spirit who promises to guide believers into all truth and to make that truth burn inside them. Facts inform, but only the Spirit transforms, and that is what is missing when the Spirit's illumination is not present.

Five Practical Implications of the Spirit's Illumination for Preaching

1. Illumination Overcomes Sin's Residue

Why do we as preachers need the Spirit's work of illumination? The direct answer is that we are still living with the effects of sin.

The depravity of our minds is still with us. That is why Paul tells us in Romans 12:1–2 to be transformed by the renewing of our minds. The Spirit is God's gracious gift to us to lead us in this transformation of the mind so that we can understand, embrace, and obey God's Word through the power of his Spirit. We must allow the Spirit's illumination to guide us when we read the Word, so our minds are not clouded by sin, doubt, or disobedience.

Apart from the Spirit's conviction and enablement, my sinful response to the power of the Word of God is to reject it, to run from it, to try to make it apply to somebody else. But when the Spirit is actively guiding me into all truth, he takes his living and active Word and deeply cuts my heart and deeply penetrates my mind, so much so that I cannot escape its transformative power, its compelling truth, its wonderful promise, and its glorious light. Though an unbeliever can figure out what the text says, he remains cold. Only a born-again believer who is sealed and filled with the Holy Spirit can experience the intense heat as he spends time in the furnace of God's Word. This is why Paul tells us not to put out the Spirit's fire (1 Thess. 5:19), and why he told young Timothy to fan into flame the gift of God (2 Tim. 1:6).

A direct correlation exists between the Spirit's illuminating ministry of Scripture and the spiritual temperature of our hearts as believers. This is why we must persevere in the spiritual disciplines of prayer and meditation. These disciplines sharpen our receptivity of the Spirit's illumination, which will serve to sharpen our preaching. This is also why the primary goal of the Spirit's illumination is not to give us something to preach; the primary goal of the Spirit's illumination is our sanctification. Let the Spirit sanctify you through the Word, and you will never lack something to preach!

Just in case you were wondering, the Spirit's illumination and exegetical sweat are not polar opposites. The Spirit's illumination does not give us an excuse to take our notes from hermeneutics class and toss them in the trash can. The "I don't need to study; I just need the Spirit" attitude is misleading because it implies that the Spirit's illumination circumvents or bypasses the classic disciplines of languages, hermeneutics, and biblical studies. Instead of working against these disciplines, the Spirit works in conjunction with these disciplines to give us not only a clear understanding of God's Word but also a passionate understanding of the significance of God's Word. I believe that any resource or tool that helps us more fully understand and appreciate the meaning of the biblical text honors the Holy Spirit.

One temptation we face as preachers is to fall in love with the tools and the process of exposition, to the degree that we become sermon factories and preaching machines. We get more excited about opening up our favorite commentary than we do about praying over the biblical text and meditating on its powerful truth. We focus more on trying to get our outlines to alliterate than we do for the Holy Spirit to illuminate. We begin to worship the process rather than the person who has saved us, Jesus Christ. Let me caution you not to make an idol out of your preparation time or your preaching. Spirit-led preaching by design helps us keep the emphasis on the Spirit, not on the sermon manuscript you think might be up for an Oscar in the category of creative beauty. My prayer for all preachers is that we fall more deeply in love with God than we do with the act of preaching.

How do we avoid falling in love with our own preaching? One way is to cultivate a heart that has been transformed by God's grace and a spirit that is broken, humble, and submissive before the Word of God. The psalmist reminds us, "The sacrifices of God are a broken spirit; a broken and contrite heart, O God, you will not despise" (Ps. 51:17). Opening up the Bible to read, study, and preach can become a cold and lifeless affair because we are constantly handling the Bible. We must remember that the Bible is not a kind of practice cadaver that we coldly and carelessly cut open with our exegetical instruments each week. Rather, it is "living" and requires us to spiritually scrub in through prayer, repentance, and confession before we take a closer look at it.

Our approach to the Word of God must be marked by a deep conviction about the gravity and the burden of the Word of God. We should pause and through prayer express to God how unworthy we are to open it and study it, much less proclaim it. The preacher needs the Holy Spirit's illumination to overcome the darkness of his own mind and the sinfulness of his own heart in order to clearly perceive, passionately embrace, and boldly proclaim the eternal truth of God's Word.

2. Illumination Transports Us into the Text

A second way we benefit from the Spirit's illumination is through identification. The Holy Spirit's light helps us as preachers to enter into the text of Scripture and to empathize and visualize what is going on in the text. When we are illuminated by the Spirit, it is as if we are inside a cave which represents God's Word, and the Spirit is our high-beam flashlight who illumines the contents of the cave so that we can see everything and take note of what the cave looks like inside. Preaching is the firsthand report or eyewitness account the preacher gives to the congregation of what the text looks like and what God expects as a result of seeing it, believing it, and experiencing it.

For example, when we hear David crying out in Psalm 51 for forgiveness, we can identify with him because we know what it is like to sin and feel dirty before God. When we see Jonah running away from the Lord's command to go to Nineveh, we can identify because we ourselves have done some running of our own. When we read Moses' excuses before the Lord when God calls him to speak before the nation, we can identify with him because we know what it's like to feel inadequate for the task God has put before us. When we hear Martha lamenting to Jesus about her sister's lack of help in the kitchen, we can identify with her because we know what it's like when serving Jesus gets in the way of being with Jesus.

Calvin calls this phenomenon "imprinting": "By receiving it [the text] with the full consent of our conscience, as truth comes down from heaven, submitting ourselves to it in right obedience, loving it with true affection by having it imprinted in our hearts, we may follow it entirely and conform ourselves to it."[2] Whether you preach with notes or without notes, one thing is certain: you must have the text imprinted on your heart before you stand up to preach. Spirit-led preaching comes from a Spirit-imprinted heart.

---

2. *Geneva Catechism*, quoted in T. F. Torrance, *The School of Faith* (London: J. Clark, 1959), Question 302.

3. Illumination Gives Birth to Further Illumination

A third benefit of the Spirit's illumination is that obedience to present illumination results in further illumination. God is looking for preachers who will linger long in the Word and saturate themselves in the Word by memorizing, meditating, and obeying Scriptures. How else can the Spirit bring a verse to your mind during the heat of the moment of delivering your sermon if you have not first placed the verse in your memory supply warehouse? Quick drive-by exegesis results in shallow drive-through sermons that leave people spiritually malnourished and hungry. Why settle for a quick exegetical snack when by diligent study and the Spirit's illumination you can serve up a satisfying four-course meal?

Preachers who respond to the Spirit's insights into God's Word and who faithfully proclaim God's message can expect to receive more of the Spirit's light. Present obedience to illumination procures future illumination. The opposite is also true: If you do not respond to the Spirit's illumination because sin has darkened your heart, then less light is given. So do not neglect the light the Spirit gives you.

4. Illumination Helps Us Know What to Emphasize

A fourth way the Spirit's illumination helps the preacher is in knowing what to emphasize and to bring into a particular message. What the preacher receives from the Holy Spirit's illumination in the study should form the content of the biblical truth he will preach. Going back to our definition of preaching reminds us that the content of our preaching is not up for debate or discussion. We preach biblical truth derived from the illuminating guidance of the Holy Spirit. The young preacher soon realizes with some frustration that he cannot bring every piece of his preparation work into the pulpit for preaching. He must choose what best helps him to express the meaning of the text. But he also needs to factor in the Spirit's illumination to his own heart as he was studying the text.

> What the Spirit illumines in the study, he will empower in the pulpit.

The preacher knows what to bring with him into the pulpit on Sunday because he experienced the Spirit's illuminating ministry all week long. Very plainly, whatever the Spirit illumines in the study, he will empower in the pulpit. Wherever the objective truth of the Word is brought alive through the subjective illumination of the Holy Spirit, the preacher will find plenty to emphasize in his message. What is bright light in the study will be white hot in the sanctuary.

5. Illumination Ignites Passion in the Pulpit

If you did not like the academic definition of illumination I gave earlier in the chapter, let me share with you another definition: The Spirit's illumination is the light that starts a fire in the preacher's study that blazes into a burning passion in the pulpit. I like to think of the Holy Spirit furnishing the intense heat of the text I am studying. Fire is something that we see, but heat is something we feel. When I read of the inseparable love of God that I have in Christ Jesus in Romans 8, when I read that nothing in heaven or on earth or in all creation can separate me from his love, my heart is warmed and gripped by the power of God's love. It stirs something inside me and causes me to want to pray and thank God. The Holy Spirit keeps preaching from becoming nothing more than a brain-oriented endeavor. Deep, clear thinking is essential to preaching, but it will turn into a dry-as-dust lecture unless the Spirit's illumination ignites fire in the preacher's soul. With the Holy Spirit's illumination, the preacher's Bible study becomes a passionate engagement with the truth of God that stirs his soul and changes his life.

One of the prayers I challenge my students to pray before they study for a message is found in Psalm 119:18: "Open my eyes that I may see wonderful things in your law." One student took me up on the challenge and sent me the e-mail below. I pray it will encourage your heart as much as it did mine.

```
Hey Dr. Heisler,

    I just needed to e-mail you because my wife
was getting tired of me saying, "Amen!, thank you
Jesus!"
    Ever since you gave your sermon preparation
class (college) our sermon manuscript texts, I
have been praying that God would reveal to me what
he was saying through this text (Mark 2:1-12) in
his inspired Holy Word. Well, I have spoken to
```

you about this text more than once and have been reading it over and over and really wrestling with what God has to say to us through this passage.

Today, 14 Nov 2005, nearly three months since I first received it, God has graciously illumined to me what he has to say through Mark 2:1—12.

Wow!! I am so excited, and I can't tell anyone exactly what I am feeling inside. Hence this bizarre e-mail to you.

But today I began by spending time with the Lord in prayer, and knowing that this afternoon I would be spending time with this passage as I begin my manuscript, I prayed for special wisdom and understanding from the Holy Spirit. Well throughout the afternoon I very carefully studied the text, and at about 6:00 p.m. the Holy Spirit whacked me over the head with the author's intended meaning.

BREAKTHRU!

God is so good!

Just when I was about to give up, God blessed me! I look forward to writing out this sermon manuscript and am now praying that I will write everything the Holy Spirit leads me to write. I look forward greatly to the day when I will be able to stand in the river of authorial intent and allow the Holy Spirit to flow through my words into hearts of people.

Well, I just wanted to say thanks! and glory to God!!

Chapter 5

Word and Spirit Together: The Theological Foundation for Spirit-Led Expository Preaching

*The Spirit of God is peculiarly precious to us, because
he especially instructs us as to the person and work of
our Lord Jesus Christ; and that is the main point of our
preaching. He takes of the things of Christ,
and shows them unto us.*

—*Charles Haddon Spurgeon*

Canoeing is not the easiest recreational sport in the world. Our missionary friends prove it every time we go. The last time we went with them, they flipped their canoe within the first thirty seconds of the journey—small kids included! This most recent incident came to us as no surprise because the first time we went canoeing with them proved beyond a shadow of a doubt their lack of canoeing expertise. We were in the mountains of Virginia vacationing together, and we had just gotten the canoes down into the water. The husband, being a gentleman, let his wife get into the canoe first. Then he pushed the canoe out away from the bank, jumped in, and started paddling. She started paddling as well.

My wife and I looked over and laughed at what we saw: Both of them sitting on opposite ends of the canoe—with their backs to each other—and each paddling in the opposite direction from the other! No wonder they weren't making any progress. And yes, just in case you are wondering, they flipped their canoe the first time we went out with them as well. Wet camera, wet lunch—you get the picture!

Some preachers see the Word and the Spirit the way we saw our canoeing friends in Virginia that day: the Word faces one way, the Spirit faces the other, and both paddle in opposite directions against each other! In this chapter we are going to see that the Word of God and the Spirit of God face the same direction in the canoe we call preaching. They even paddle in the same direction because they share the same goal—the Christological witness to Jesus Christ. They ride together down the river of the authorial intent, and our role as preachers is to ride with the Word and the Spirit as they guide us downstream.

If the Spirit's illumination is the hermeneutical foundation for Spirit-led preaching, then the theological foundation is built upon the complementary relationship between the Holy Spirit and the Word of God. This chapter is too short to be a full-fledged theology of the Spirit. Instead, this chapter will focus on the biblical and theological elements of the Holy Spirit's ministry that have a direct impact on preaching. The chapter will establish the ministry of the Holy Spirit from a biblical perspective, focusing on the Spirit as the guide to truth, the revealer of Christ, and the source of all genuine conviction.

Next, the interdependent nature of the Word and Spirit will be developed as the catalyst of Spirit-led exposition. When the Word and Spirit combine, combustion happens and power results! Spirit-led preaching thrives on the powerful and inseparable tandem of Word and Spirit. Finally, the implications of the theological categories of Word and Spirit will be applied to preaching.

Biblical Foundation

Jesus previewed the ministry of the Holy Spirit in John's Gospel. He said in John 14:16–17, "And I will ask the Father, and he will give you another Counselor to be with you forever—the Spirit of truth." Jesus identified the Holy Spirit in this passage as the Spirit of truth. The Spirit of truth is sent by the Father at the request of the Son and indwells believers as a resident minister who guides us into all truth. Jesus elaborated on the Spirit as the guide into all truth when he said in John 16:13, "But when he, the Spirit of truth, comes, he will guide you into all truth. He will not speak on his own; he will speak only what he hears, and he will tell you what is yet to come."

Notice that Jesus limited the Spirit's leadership into all truth to "what he [the Spirit] hears." We might ask, "What does the Spirit hear?" Jesus answered that very question in the same passage in John 16 when he said, "He will bring glory to me by taking from what is mine and making it known to you. All that belongs to the Father is mine. That is why I said the Spirit will take from what is mine and make it known to you" (John 16:14–15). Jesus identified the Spirit's ministry as a continuation of his own ministry; in fact, the text indicates that the Holy Spirit is of the same kind (deity) as Jesus. Therefore, the Spirit hears and applies to us Jesus. The Spirit reveals and glorifies Christ by magnifying Christ's teaching, Christ's gospel, and Christ's work as the grand fulfillment of God's redemptive plan. The Bible is a united testimony to Jesus Christ, and the Spirit's joy is giving witness to this testimony and making it known to us. Spirit-led preaching comes into alignment with the Spirit's ministry of glorifying Jesus Christ by proclaiming the written Word in order to glorify the living Word.

In addition to guiding us into all the truth, the Spirit also convicts us of the truth. Again, Jesus teaches us about the Spirit's conviction when he states the Spirit "will convict the world of guilt in regard to sin and righteousness and judgment" (John 16:8). The Greek word for convict is *elencho,* which means to "bring to light," "expose," "set forth," "convince," "punish," and "discipline." The Spirit's conviction operates in the realm of unbelief, righteousness, and judgment, all of which align perfectly with the great themes of the gospel of Jesus Christ. We believe because the Spirit convicts us that what we are hearing is true. We repent because the Spirit convicts us that we have sin in our lives. We walk in righteousness because the Spirit convicts us that we will face a righteous and just judgment. Hence, the Spirit of God accompanies the Word of God in order to produce conviction in those who hear it. The biblical evidence clearly points to the Holy Spirit's ministry as the Spirit of truth, the revealer of Jesus Christ, and the source of all genuine conviction.

Spirit of Truth: *Testimonium*

Theologians, in clarifying the work of the Holy Spirit as the guide into all truth, have used the Latin term *testimonium spiritus sancti internum* (inner testimony of the Holy Spirit) to refer to the witnessing ministry of the Holy Spirit. John Calvin, known as the theologian of the Holy Spirit, defined the Spirit's *testimonium* as the "efficacious confirmation of the Word."[1] The idea behind the *testimonium* is that the Holy Spirit's testimony concerning Scripture affirms the trustworthiness of the Bible (you can believe this) and the urgent need for receptivity (you should obey this). The Spirit's internal witness does not *make* Scripture authoritative in a Barthian or neo-orthodox understanding; rather, the Spirit testifies to the Scriptures' inherent inspiration and authority. Warfield notes, "The testimony of the Spirit is the subjective preparation of the heart to receive the objective evidence in a sympathetic embrace."[2] The Spirit's internal witness to biblical truth causes us to give unwavering assent to its truthfulness and puts a desire in our heart to submit to it.

This is a good place to raise an important question for preaching: Where does the preacher's confidence come from when standing to proclaim the Word of God? Some would answer that our confidence comes from God's revealed Word, the Bible. I agree wholeheartedly. In fact, the Bible does not need my assent to be true; it is true because it's the Word. I would also add that the Spirit's quickening of the Word to my own heart—his *testimonium* in my own heart—is also reason to stand and preach with confidence and boldness. I have *both* the God-breathed, 2 Timothy 3:16-inspired Scriptures; and I also have the Spirit-illumined Psalm 119:18 *testimonium*. Second Timothy 3:16 is my objective truth (Word), and Psalm 119:18 is my subjective confirmation (Spirit). I believe the Bible is true because it claims to be true, and I believe the Bible is true because it continues to change my life.

---

1. John Calvin, *The Institutes of the Christian Religion*, 1.9.3, trans. Henry Beveridge, in QuickVerse 7.0 [CD-ROM] (Omaha, Neb.: Parsons Church Group, 2001).

2. B. B. Warfield, *Calvin and Augustine* (Philadelphia: Presbyterian and Reformed, 1965), 74.

The most powerful preaching on earth happens when we preach out of a heart that has been deeply and profoundly affected by the truth of the Word. Sometimes one of my students moves out of his "preacher mode" and says something like, "Guys, God really convicted me with this text and spoke to my heart as I was preparing this message. I just want to share my heart with you for the next minute or two." When I hear something along those lines, I sit up and take notice. Why? I am about to experience what I call heart-to-heart preaching, spirit-to-spirit preaching, one soul preaching to another soul—by way of the Holy Spirit. No more abstract thoughts, no more theory—this is testimony! This is where the Spirit's *testimonium* was white hot in that student's life, and I know what he is about to say was birthed in the deep furnace of his soul in response to the Spirit's work as he pored over that text in prayerful study.

Revealer of Christ Alone

Jesus instructed his disciples that when the Holy Spirit came, he would "testify about me" (John 15:26). The Spirit's ministry is a continuation of Jesus' ministry, as the Spirit stands in place of Jesus until Christ's triumphant return. In the meantime the Spirit's role is to infiltrate the sinful world and confront people with the power of the gospel. Just as Jesus revealed the Father to us, so the Spirit's role is to reveal the Son, who reveals the Father. This is why we need a robust trinitarian theology informing our understanding of biblical preaching. The Spirit rejoices to place all attention and focus on the magnification of Jesus Christ as Lord. That's why Jesus said in John 16:14 that the Spirit is not interested in his own glory: "He will bring glory to me by taking from what is mine and making it known to you."

One reason so much of what is done in the name of the Holy Spirit today is not of the Spirit is because Jesus is never mentioned or glorified. That contradicts Jesus' teaching and should warn us as preachers that our sermons must be Christ centered and redemptive in their focus, or the Spirit's power will have nothing to do with them. As Spirit-filled preachers deliver their messages, the Holy Spirit bears witness to the incarnate Word through the written Word.

Let me give you a practical example of how theology informs methodology. In Acts 16, the Bible says that Paul was speaking to a group of women outside the city of Philippi. One of those listening was Lydia, who went on to become one of the great supporters of the apostle's ministry. In the process of Paul's speaking, "the Lord opened her heart to respond to Paul's message" (Acts 16:14). Paul spoke, but the Lord opened her heart.

One of the mistakes I made early in my preaching ministry was to put an undue pressure on myself by trying to figure out how best to get the hearts of my people to open up: a tear-jerker story at just the right place, a shocking statistic, or a surprise ending that nobody sees coming. Yet this passage reminds us as preachers that the ultimate persuasion is the Spirit's persuasion. Sometimes we overemphasize human rhetoric to the degree that we begin to think we are the persuaders of truth. But if the Spirit convinces, if the Spirit convicts, and if the Spirit opens the heart, then people leave with their faith in God's Word and God's Spirit, "so that your faith might not rest on men's wisdom, but on God's power" (1 Cor. 2:5).

Whether God chooses to open hearts and pull back the scales of unbelief is his sovereign ministry through the Spirit. I pray intensely and fervently that it will happen every time I preach, but I cannot *make* it happen. My calling is to preach, and I dare not put my confidence in anything other than the power of the Word of God and the Spirit's illumination of the Word of God to open hearts darkened by sin.

Whenever you preach, give the Spirit something he can testify to. Spirit-led preaching calls us to give the Spirit something he can work with when we preach. He's not interested in working with our vacillating opinions, our petty preferences, our feel-good stories, or our color commentary on current events. Instead, preach Scripture, and the Spirit will always have something to testify to in your message, and you will never have to doubt whether you are preaching something the Spirit wants you to preach. Preaching that remains within the bounds of the biblical text is most likely to receive the benefits of the revealing ministry of the Holy Spirit. The Spirit's testimonium—the Spirit as revealer of Christ—is tied to Scripture. Jesus said, "These are the Scriptures that testify of me!" When Jesus wanted to reveal himself to the disciples on the road to Emmaus, he used Scripture. If my goal is for people to see the Savior when I preach, then my obligation is to partner with the Holy Spirit so I can *preach Christ* to my audience and the Spirit can at the same time *reveal Christ* to my audience.

When I preach Scripture, I come into alignment with the themes that the Spirit implanted in the biblical text. Jesus taught in John 16:13–15 that the Spirit's conviction is specific and centers on the themes of sin, righteousness, and judgment. The Spirit's conviction is for both believers and unbelievers. For believers the Holy Spirit glorifies Christ by convicting the believer of sins committed, of righteousness imputed, and of judgment accomplished. For unbelievers the Spirit's work focuses on convincing sinners of their separation from God, the futility of self-righteousness for salvation, and the just judgment of God.

For example, the apostle Paul serves as a great model for preaching themes that tie into the Spirit's ministry of conviction. In Acts 24, Paul's preaching is outlined for us:

> Several days later Felix came with his wife Drusilla, who was a Jewess. He sent for Paul and listened to him as he spoke about faith in Christ Jesus. As Paul discoursed on righteousness, self-control and the judgment to come, Felix was afraid and said, "That's enough for now! You may leave. When I find it convenient, I will send for you" (Acts 24:24–25).

First of all, notice that Paul was preaching the gospel to Felix: "as he spoke about faith in Christ Jesus." The preacher's first and greatest concern is that his preaching testifies to Jesus Christ and his gospel. Second, notice Paul's three main points: righteousness, self-control, and judgment. Do two of those sound familiar? If we understand that a lack of self-control is the root of sin, then we have the three pillars of the Holy Spirit's conviction: sin, righteousness, and judgment. No wonder Felix was afraid. He was experiencing the conviction of the Holy Spirit! When we preach "the Scriptures that testify about me" (John 5:39), our preaching will be bathed in the biblical themes of sin, righteousness, and the judgment to come. This is why we must preach the Word of God as it is, without backing away from or watering down the hard and penetrating truths concerning sin, righteousness, and the judgment to come. Paul could have easily tickled Felix's ears in hopes of being released, but instead he was emboldened by the Spirit to bring Felix face-to-face with his sin.

Is it possible that we see so few people saved from our preaching because we no longer preach these themes from the Bible? Has the sensitized and sanitized contemporary pulpit moved beyond these biblical themes and embraced more culturally acceptable, politically correct, and less offensive themes? Such nonconfrontational preaching may leave people feeling better about themselves, but it also leaves them just as lost as they were when they walked through the door of the church. If you don't take anything else away from this chapter, please get this: the Holy Spirit of God is confrontational, and his conviction is powerful. He will not empower nonconfrontational preaching that waters down the gospel, compromises the Word, and takes sin lightly.

I believe we are grieving and quenching the Holy Spirit when we say less than what the Bible says in an effort not to offend anyone or more than the Bible says in order to impress everyone. The reality is that we are offending someone—the Holy Spirit—and he is not impressed! Preaching that is soft on sin and fearful of confronting people reveals that we prefer the Spirit of God who *comforts* us but run from the Spirit who *convicts* us.

Spirit-led preaching calls us to align our preaching with the ministries of the Holy Spirit revealed in Scripture. It is as if the Spirit says to us as preachers, "Here I am. Here's what I am commissioned by Jesus to do. Study me. Know what I am capable of, and know what I testify to. I have called you to preach God's Word, and I want you to join me as I bring Christ glory by revealing him to others. You must make a commitment to me that you will preach my Spirit-inspired Word in the power I will give you." I know this is an imaginary conversation, but at least it helps me to be aware of what the Spirit offers for preaching and his desire to work in and through me. It also reminds me that the Holy Spirit is a person and not some impersonal force. It also relieves me because I am not the one responsible for changing lives and opening hearts; the Spirit is. Only the truth of

God's Word combined with the convicting power of the Holy Spirit can change lives for all eternity. Not my creativity or ingenuity as a preacher. Not my loud voice or my dynamic delivery. Not the poetic beauty or perfect symmetry of my well-crafted sermon. The truth of the Word and the power of the Spirit—that's our hope!

Word and Spirit in Combination

The Word of God and Spirit of God share a dynamic relationship of interdependence. I like to think of them together, like the two sides of a single coin. Ezekiel 37 is particularly helpful at demonstrating this relationship. The context of Ezekiel 37 is Israel's disobedience that had led to their spiritual death as a nation. God's prophet was called upon to contemplate the possibility of resurrecting a nation that was dead toward God. God questioned the prophet if the nation was beyond hope: "Son of man, can these bones live?" (Ezek. 37:3). The situation was so grave that it was even beyond Ezekiel's capacity to speculate. He responded by telling Yahweh that only he as the Lord God knew the answer.

In verse 4 God commanded Ezekiel to preach: "Prophesy to these bones." Prophecy in this context refers to the declaration of the Word of the Lord. So God taught Ezekiel that resurrection life begins with the prophetic Word proclaimed. Just as an aside, if you think preaching to your congregation is like preaching to the dead, imagine Ezekiel! OK, bad joke—back to the story. The effect of the Word was immediate and powerful: "The bones came together, bone to bone" (Ezek. 37:7). If the story ended there, all we would have is an army of lifeless skeletons. Next God told Ezekiel that something was missing: the spirit or *ruach,* that is, God's life-giving breath! So Ezekiel called forth the Spirit to breathe life into the skeletons, and by the power of the Word and by the power of the Spirit, "they came to life and stood up on their feet" (Ezek. 37:10).

Ezekiel 37 states the Spirit's role clearly: "to breathe into." What the Spirit breathes life into comes alive. This concept of the Spirit's "breathing into" is a foreshadowing of the breathing taking place in 2 Timothy 3:16 where the Bible says that all Scripture is "God-breathed." The Spirit's "life-giving breath" is why Hebrews 4:12 can speak of the Bible as being living and active. The Spirit of God and the Word of God are not antagonistic, and any attempt to put them at odds is unbiblical and theologically irresponsible. Instead, we find in both the Old Testament and the New Testament that the Word of God and the Spirit of God are in constant, continuous, and complementary relationship to each other.

Together Word and Spirit form the powerful catalyst that serves as the theological foundation for Spirit-led preaching. The Word activates the Spirit, and the Spirit authenticates the Word. The Word is the instrument of the Spirit, and the Spirit is the implement of the Word. The Word is the written witness, and the Spirit is the inward witness. In terms of preaching, the Word is the source and substance of our preaching, and the Spirit is the supernatural power of our preaching.

Since the Word and Spirit depend on and thrive on each other, Spirit-led preachers must reject the notion that we must somehow "balance" these two theological realities. We do not seek to balance the Word with the Spirit or the Spirit with the Word. Instead we seek to be filled with the Spirit and to be saturated with the Word simultaneously and abundantly. The Word and Spirit are not enemies but colaborers in Christ. As a preacher, I want both to be working with me, in me, and through me as I preach.

Word and Spirit Together: Christological Preaching

The implications of the Spirit's biblically defined ministry combined with the theological relationship between the Word and the Spirit demand Christ-centered preaching. The biblical and theological foundation for Word-and-Spirit preaching is seen in the following emphases.

The Scriptures Are Christ Centered.

- "You diligently study the Scriptures because you think that by them you possess eternal life. These are the Scriptures that testify about me" (John 5:39).
- "And beginning with Moses and all the Prophets, he explained to them what was said in all the Scriptures concerning himself" (Luke 24:27).

- "Jesus did many other miraculous signs in the presence disciples, which are not recorded in this book. But thes written that you may believe that Jesus is the Christ, the Son of God, and that by believing you may have life in his name" (John 20:30–31).

The Spirit Is Christ Centered.

- "But the Counselor, the Holy Spirit, whom the Father will send in my name, will teach you all things and will remind you of everything I have said to you" (John 14:26).
- "When the Counselor comes, whom I will send to you from the Father, the Spirit of truth who goes out from the Father, he will testify about me" (John 15:26).
- "But when he, the Spirit of truth, comes, he will guide you into all truth. . . . He will bring glory to me by taking from what is mine and making it known to you" (John 16:13–14).

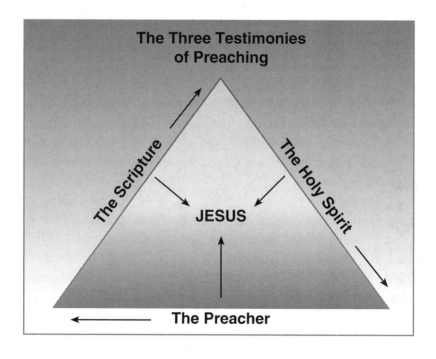

The Preacher Is Christ Centered.

- "For we do not preach ourselves, but Jesus Christ as Lord" (2 Cor. 4:5).
- "Boldly and without hindrance he preached the kingdom of God and taught about the Lord Jesus Christ" (Acts 28:31).
- "But we preach Christ crucified" (1 Cor. 1:23).

These three categories form a powerful foundation for Spirit-led preaching. I like to refer to them as the three witnesses of preaching or the three testimonies of preaching. The diagram below visually represents the dynamic of Spirit-led preaching as the Word, the Spirit, and the preacher all testify to Christ.

If you begin on the diagram with the preacher and move clockwise, you recognize this pattern: the Spirit-empowered preacher preaches the Spirit-inspired Scriptures, pointing at all times to the centrality of the person and work of Jesus Christ. Spirit-led preaching happens when the Word, the Spirit, and the preacher all testify to Jesus Christ in a unified and powerful witness.

As the Word and the Spirit combine to give witness to Jesus Christ, it is incumbent upon the preacher to join in that witness by preaching Christ as well. By preaching Christ, I mean that every sermon should be redemptive in focus and should *by design,* not by accident, draw attention to the person and the work of Jesus Christ. Simply throwing Christ into the mix at some point along the way in our message is not honoring to Christ, the text, or the Spirit. If Jesus only comes up during the last forty seconds of your message when you say, "If you are here and you've never trusted Christ before . . . ," your preaching is not Christological by any stretch of the imagination.

Christological preaching happens when we build the theological component of our message upon one significant question: How does this text testify to the person and work of Jesus Christ? Whether preaching in the Old Testament or in the New Testament, we should constantly seek to understand how Christ's death, burial, and resurrection fulfill the redemptive focus of the text that we are preaching. This means that Spirit-led preaching is by definition evangelical preaching and will always seek a Christ-specific response.

May I take a moment to encourage you as a preacher? Don't believe everything you read about what people want to hear when they come to church. The opinion of the pew should not determine the content of the pulpit. I have found that Spirit-led, transformational preaching—preaching that points people to Christ's redemptive power, preaching that unashamedly calls for a faith response, preaching that stays "on message" with the Spirit-intended meaning of the text, preaching that magnifies the life-changing gospel of Jesus Christ—feeds the flock and fires up the sheep.

Throw away those surveys that tell you what people want to hear when they come to church. Preach the Bible with clarity and conviction in the power of the Spirit. Paul never told Timothy, "Survey the people, and see what they want to hear." Instead he warned, "For the time will come when men will not put up with sound doctrine. Instead, to suit their own desires, they will gather around them a great number of teachers to say what their itching ears want to hear" (2 Tim. 4:3).

Recently during an evening worship service at a church where I was preaching, I was unexpectedly approached during the middle of a worship song by a middle-aged mother. I was a little caught off guard by her timing; but then again when people get burdened for lost souls, following the Spirit is more important than following the rules of worship etiquette. I stopped singing and leaned toward her so I could hear her. "I was here this morning, and I heard your message on the rich young ruler," she said. "I knew you were going to be preaching the same message again tonight, so I brought my teenage son back with me. He's not a believer, and I'm afraid if he doesn't hear this message and respond tonight, he's going to walk away like the rich young ruler did. I just wanted you to know that he's here and I'm praying." And then she just walked back into the crowd.

"He's here, and I'm praying." What a powerful reminder of why we preach! What a wake-up call to us as preachers! I was convicted in a powerful way that night of what's at stake every time we preach. Richard Baxter captured the intensity every preacher should sense when he said, "I preach as a dying man to dying men." God challenged me to sense and feel the urgency of the gospel and the burden of preaching. Like a wake-up call from God, the Lord reminded me through this woman's divine interruption that every time I preach, there's a mom or a dad counting on me to deliver the truth in the power of the Holy Spirit.

I don't know how many times you've been interrupted with that kind of message before you've preached, but my prayer is that the Holy Spirit would remind you of the lostness of humanity every time you preach. After she shared her burden, I didn't feel like singing anymore. My mind was suddenly preoccupied with eternity, and I believe that's the way it should be before we preach. All I wanted to do was pray for this mother's teenage son—and others like him— that the Spirit of God would open his heart to the truth of the gospel, that he would be saved.

In a fresh way that night, God shook me out of my routine and reminded me that I preach Jesus so that others can believe on him, call on his name, and be saved. My message must give witness to Christ and the gospel. I must have the power of the Holy Spirit accompany me when I preach. I must preach as a man fully surrendered to Christ. I must preach as a man under divine compulsion. I cannot keep silent. I cannot listen to the evil one who whispers to me, "Do you have to preach Christ in every sermon?" Moms are burdened and praying. Teenage sons are lost and dying. And you stand to preach.

Every week before you preach, pray and ask the Holy Spirit to place you under the burden of preaching as you meditate on this text: "How, then, can they call on the one they have not believed in? And how can they believe in the one of whom they have not heard? And how can they hear without someone preaching to them?" (Rom. 10:14). Let me encourage you to take a few minutes and meditate on the above Scripture as we end this chapter. Ask the Holy Spirit to burn into your heart the burden for lost souls to come to Christ through the preaching of his cross.

Chapter 6

The Spirit and the
Preacher's Sanctification

*Where preachers are intent
on glorifying Christ, the Spirit is there
with all His aid. Only crucified men
can speak of a crucified Savior.*

—William Still

On a recent stop at the gas station, a sign by the pump caught my eye. I had read the sign many times before and had become quite adept at ignoring it. The sign read: "Warning! To avoid risk, only pump gas into preapproved containers." I know the sign was basically telling me that not everything is fit for holding gas. Gas is explosive and flammable, and it should be stored in the proper container. A proper container is one that is designed to hold or transport gas.

When it comes to the Holy Spirit and preaching, I believe God puts a similar warning sign on the container that transports the Word and the Spirit: "Warning! To avoid risk, only preach from pure and holy containers that are approved by God." Spirit-led preaching views the preacher as the vessel or container that transports the Word and the Spirit to the congregation and then delivers what's inside. But the Bible is clear that not just any container will suffice. It must be "preapproved" by the Lord. Titus 1:7 states, "Since an overseer is entrusted with God's work, he must be blameless." God's preapproved container must be holy, pure, and above reproach. Just as the structural integrity of a building must be designed to bear the weight of the building, so the structural integrity of the preacher— his character and integrity—must be able to transport the holy Word of God and the Holy Spirit of God to the people of God.

Preachers who are saturated in the Scriptures and filled by the Spirit need a new warning label as they preach: "Caution! Highly flammable and theologically combustible. Contents can radically alter your life. Listen carefully and use only as the Spirit convicts you." Do you think people in the pew would listen differently if you began your sermon with that disclaimer next Sunday? Do you as God's preacher take for granted just how powerful the Word of God is? When the Spirit of God and the Word of God are mixed together inside a preacher's heart and are together proclaimed out of his mouth, powerful, Spirit-led preaching takes place. In this chapter, we examine the preacher as the vessel who delivers the Word of God in the power of the Spirit of God.

Preaching is much like an iceberg. What people see in the pulpit on Sunday is the tip of the dynamics going on beneath the surface. Beneath the surface, the Spirit of God is at work in the preacher's life long before eleven o'clock on Sunday morning. Spirit-led preaching approaches the Spirit holistically because the Spirit penetrates every aspect of our lives. Therefore, Spirit-filled living is God's prerequisite for Spirit-led preaching.

Beginning at conversion, the Holy Spirit becomes a daily reality in our lives as we seek to understand and submit to his role as sanctifier of our lives. Our call to preach, the formation of our character, and the preparation we undergo for ministry involve the Spirit's leadership. The Spirit of God molds and makes the preacher long before the preacher molds and makes a sermon. The Spirit of God continues to mold and make the preacher long after the sermon is delivered.

The practical implications of Spirit-led preaching begin with this foundational truth: the Holy Spirit's power for preaching is grounded in the *process* of spiritual sanctification. Being Spirit led and Spirit filled is grounded in the vital relationship we have with the Spirit, whose mission is to transform us and to mature us into Christlikeness. This means that if we are not Spirit led and Spirit filled in our homes and in our communities, we should not anticipate being Spirit led and Spirit filled in the pulpit. Our first calling is to keep growing spiritually while bearing the Spirit's fruit and then to approach preaching as an outgrowth of the vitality of the Spirit.

The Conversion of the Preacher

Beginning with our conversion to faith in Christ may seem like a strange place to start, since most books on preaching assume their readers are Christians. Yet there can be no Spirit-led preaching unless you as a preacher are completely confident that the indwelling Holy Spirit of God resides inside you on a permanent basis. I believe the Bible teaches in Ephesians 1:13 that we receive the Holy Spirit at conversion when we believe and are "marked in him with a seal." So before our preaching can be Spirit filled, our souls must be Spirit sealed.

Conversion is important because it is also our first experience of the Holy Spirit. It's because we heard the Word of God and because we experienced the conviction of the Holy Spirit, that we repented and believed. This initial experience of the Spirit's work of regeneration within us is powerful because it marks us for life. We cannot approach preaching without it.

For example, can you imagine the apostle Paul preaching the gospel and being forced by his homiletics professor never to mention his conversion experience during his message? Of course not! In fact, Paul continually went back to his conversion as the source of his preaching and missionary activity. He testified that he was "shown mercy . . . as an example" for those who would believe on Jesus and receive eternal life (1 Tim. 1:15–16). The apostle Paul testified, "But when God, who set me apart from birth and called me by his grace, was pleased to reveal his Son in me so that I might preach him" (Gal. 1:15–16). Notice the call to preach ("so that I might preach him") is preceded by the call to salvation ("called me by his grace/pleased to reveal his Son in me"). We preach because we have been redeemed. We preach because we have been shown mercy. Our conversion experience leaves such an unforgettable impression upon our hearts and minds that it continuously spills over into our preaching.

Testimony is a key ingredient of Spirit-led preaching because the most powerful preachers I know have never gotten over the wonder and the joy of their salvation experience. Every time they preach, they preach as if they just heard the good news the night before and cannot wait to say, like the blind man in John 9:25, "One thing I do know. I was blind but now I see!"

Conversion, Faith, and the Spirit's Seal

Not only is conversion a demonstration of the power of the Holy Spirit, but it also results in believing faith. Paul declared, "No one can say, 'Jesus is Lord,' except by the Holy Spirit" (1 Cor. 12:3). Salvation is a gift from God and is only received by faith, according to Ephesians 2:8–9. In much the same way, preaching is a gift and must be exercised in faith. Paul said, "No one can say, 'Jesus is Lord,' except by the Holy Spirit," and I would add that no one can preach "Jesus is Lord" except by God's Spirit.

Every time we stand in a pulpit, open a Bible, pray, and preach, we are exercising faith: we believe that the Spirit who inspired the Word of God and who illumined the Word of God to us will now proclaim the Word of God through us so that people will hear God speaking through us. Talk about the need for faith! We can come to the pulpit with fear and trembling; we can come to the pulpit with anguished hearts; we can come to the pulpit in awe of the God we serve, but we dare not come to the pulpit in unbelief! Just as we trust God for our salvation, we trust God for our preaching.

One grace that helps us approach preaching in faith is the fact that we are sealed with the Holy Spirit as New Testament believers. Ephesians 1:13 reminds us that "having believed, you were marked in him with a seal, the promised Holy Spirit." Ephesians 4:30 warns us not to grieve the Spirit, "with whom you were sealed for the day of redemption." This "marking" and "sealing" is reassuring to me both as a believer and as a preacher because it reminds me that God has placed the power plant for preaching right inside us. I have a resident instructor and guide to the Bible. The author of Scripture resides inside me, and he can help me overcome all my human inadequacies and personal weaknesses as I prepare and deliver his

Word. When I stand to preach, I believe by faith that the Spirit who lives within me will empower me and guide me.

The Call of the Preacher

The fact that a person is saved and converted does not make him an automatic candidate for the pulpit. Spirit-led preaching can only be undertaken by a Spirit-called preacher. First, there must be a divine call to preach that is firmly grounded in God's sovereign initiative, and that comes through the Spirit's inward prompting. Someone who hears and responds to God's call can say, "I did not choose preaching; preaching chose me."

One of the problems caused by the fall of so many prominent ministers in recent years is that people became convinced that men were choosing the ministry the way people sometimes choose a profession—to make the most money. Professions are careers that people choose; preaching is a calling to which we surrender. We do not preach because we have nothing else to do; we preach because the call of God will not allow us to do anything else.

I experienced that call while attending seminary in 1996. I had arrived at seminary eager to learn and ready to serve, but I was unclear about how and where to serve God. At seminary that I met a man who walked with God, and his name was Robert Smith. He was my preaching professor, but more than that he was my Eli who taught me how to discern Gods' voice. He knew God was dealing with me and preparing to call me to preach, even before I knew it. Like Samuel I kept inquiring of him, and like Eli he kept telling me to keep praying and keep listening to the Lord. Then one morning during my devotional time, God spoke clearly to my heart through the apostle Paul's words in 1 Corinthians 9:16: "Woe to me if I do not preach the gospel!" Those words to this day serve as my call to preach.

We can drag our feet, we can delay, we can make excuses, we can take the next ship to Tarshish and run; but when God is truly dealing with you, you will have no peace until you surrender to his will for your life. If God is calling you to preach, I invite you to surrender to him even now in prayer. If you are presently doubting or questioning your call to preach, keep reading.

Calling as a Source of Confidence

The surest way to a powerless preaching ministry is to doubt God's calling. In fact, I believe that the passion and confidence the prophet of God experiences in his preaching ministry are directly proportional to the daily obedience and surrender to the call of God on the preacher's life. We must believe that when we stand and deliver God's Word to God's people, we are doing so because we have been summoned there by God himself. It's as if God has subpoenaed us to stand before him, not in a courtroom in front of a jury but in a pulpit in front of his people. We are there by divine calling, and we are there by God's authority.

One explanation for powerless preaching today is that some preachers simply lack the call. This says nothing of their character or integrity, nor does it suggest that they cannot serve God in some other capacity. I know many godly men who serve on the church staff and who serve the Lord and the church in tremendous ways, but they know they are not called to preach. Vines and Shaddix give this warning as well: "If a man goes into the ministry for any other reason than the inward prompting of the Holy Spirit, he is doing it for the wrong reason. Chances are that he will not last."[1] The preacher's "staying power" week in and week out must be grounded in a clarion call to preach the gospel. The call of God is critical because it shapes and informs the preacher's sense of identity. Preachers must know who they are in Christ, and they must be clear about the Spirit's call to ministry.

Calling as a Source of Authority

The preacher's authority as a herald sent by God comes directly from the call of God on his life and the message God gives him to preach. When someone asks, "What gives you the right to say what you say?" our response must be, "God has called and authorized me to preach his Word in the power of his Spirit to the hearts of

---

1. Jerry Vines and Jim Shaddix, *Power in the Pulpit: How to Prepare and Deliver Expository Sermons* (Chicago: Moody, 1999), 46.

his people." Preachers are appointed and anointed for their task of proclaiming the Scriptures. Now if you have already determined in your heart that you are going to speak "your word" rather than "God's Word," then you have undermined and abandoned the nature of your calling.

The herald is charged with passing on the king's message, not coming up with his own. If I deliver the message that God the Holy Spirit has given to me in Scripture, then I prove as a preacher to be faithful steward of God's Word and a man under the King's authority. This is why preaching is such a high calling and why serving as God's vessel and God's mouthpiece is tremendously humbling.

Calling as Priority

Not only do we receive authority from our calling, but we also receive the divine mandate for our ministry when we surrender to God's calling. We do not choose the focus of our ministry; it is chosen for us by the nature and responsibility of the calling. Our labor of love is cutting straight the Word of God. Our passion is being in the Lord's presence, worshipping, listening, praying, and then proclaiming what we have heard. Our power is clear: the Spirit of God, empowering the preacher of God, to boldly proclaim the Word of God. Take a minute and ask God in prayer to keep your calling clear, your passion hot, your devotion deep, your heart undivided, and your focus intense.

We must resist anything that would deter us from pursuing our divine mandate for preaching the Word of God. We must ask the Spirit of God to convict us deeply when we stray from our divine mandate to preach the Word, when we compromise our calling by endeavoring to do lesser things. In the spirit of Acts 6:4, pastors must put the preaching ministry above all other duties: we "will give our attention to prayer and the ministry of the word." A preacher cannot be pulled in a thousand different directions week in and week out and expect the power of the Spirit to show up in his sermons each week. The church needs prophets who have been in the presence of the Lord and who preach with spiritual power, not executives who run the company business. The church has plenty of busy pastors but few Spirit-filled prophets. In light of 2 Timothy 4:2, we are to preach the Word.

According to John 21:17, if we love the Lord Jesus, we will feed the lambs he has entrusted to us. Our congregations need to know that we don't preach because we are paid to preach; we preach because it expresses our love for Jesus and the sheep. Any financial help a church can supply us with is greatly appreciated because it means we can be more devoted to feeding and caring for the flock. But it is never the reason we preach. The minute we see our preaching as a reason for picking up a paycheck is the minute we need to find something else to do.

The call to preach is a continuous catalyst for Spirit-led preaching. The preacher's authority, the preacher's priority, and the preacher's passion are rooted in God's gracious call to ministry. Our experience parallels Jeremiah's: our calling from God to preach places fire in our bones with such intensity that we cannot quit preaching, and we cannot keep silent.

The Preacher's Training for Ministry

Having experienced a genuine conversion to Christ through the Holy Spirit, as well as hearing a distinctive call to preach, how should we prepare for such a calling? In the New Testament Paul instructed his young preacher Timothy, "Study to shew thyself approved unto God, a workman that needeth not to be ashamed, rightly dividing the word of truth" (2 Tim. 2:15 KJV). Studying the Word of God is a good place to start. In the Old Testament Ezra the priest serves as an example of a life devoted to preaching and teaching: "For Ezra had devoted himself to the study and observance of the Law of the LORD, and to teaching its decrees and laws in Israel" (Ezra 7:10). Although a formal seminary education is not required to fulfill the call to preach, some type of study, whether self-taught or under the tutelage of a seasoned pastor, will help the preacher know how to "rightly divide" the word of truth.

College and seminary degrees are *not* in conflict with the Holy Spirit. If the Spirit was all we needed, then Paul never would have written anything to Timothy because the Spirit alone would have been sufficient for first-century ministry. Yet what we have in 1 and 2 Timothy is essentially a first-century "Life and Work of the Pastor" class, taught by Paul and inspired by the Spirit. Education is helpful and beneficial because anything that helps us to understand and grasp the meaning of God's Word better will help us communicate it more clearly and precisely.

Education and the Spirit

If there is a danger with education, it is this: No amount of learning can substitute for the Spirit's power in preaching. Learning truth—whether through books, seminary classes, or online education—may fill our minds and hearts with knowledge, but only the Spirit of God can set us on fire! We must always keep our education and our pursuit of knowledge in proper perspective, and never let a degree or a title puff us up with pride. The man with a chip on his shoulder has no room for a cross on his back.

If you come to Southeastern Seminary in Wake Forest, North Carolina, you will see a sign outside my office that reminds me of the vision God placed on my heart when he called me to the seminary to teach preaching:

> VISION: To advance the kingdom of God by raising up a generation of God-called, Spirit-empowered, and Christ-exalting preachers who with passion and intensity rightly divide and boldly proclaim the Word of God out of the overflow of a heart set on fire by God!

I know my vision statement is a run-on sentence and is an English teacher's nightmare, but that's not the point. The point is, I need to be reminded continually that teaching preaching involves more than just five steps, seven principles, or four skills. Spiritual dynamics such as Word and Spirit, illumination and empowerment, and confession and consecration cannot go unmentioned in the classroom. I am determined in my approach to teaching preaching to keep the dynamics of the Holy Spirit at the center of the discipline of homiletics. That's why I begin each semester with a strong emphasis on the Spirit, for without the Spirit's power preaching turns into points and subpoints that end up making no point!

One of the real dangers of teaching homiletics is to teach a particular model or method that fails to incorporate the dynamic of the Spirit in the text. Instead of forcing students to learn a mechanical method, we should teach them to incarnate the Word. My own seminary experience proved the point. My homiletics classes featured textbooks that said much about breaking down the text but little about how the Spirit breaks down the preacher. Lectures taught me the history of preaching but not the Holy Spirit of preaching. To my seminary's credit a tremendous emphasis was placed on rightly dividing the Word, and for that I am grateful. We need to get the text right if our preaching is to have power. So I learned how to diagram the text. I learned how to parse verbs, execute word studies, and establish the context of a passage. I learned how to turn an exegetical outline into a homiletic outline.

Unknowingly, my training was creating in me a false understanding of preaching. I was starting to believe that preaching was all about following a certain process—complete the seven steps, follow the five rules, avoid this mistake, don't do that—to preach a great sermon. Later, after I had graduated and was beginning to think through my own approach to preaching, God impressed upon me that preaching at its heart is not about following a mechanical process every week but rather about following a person—the third person of the Trinity, to be exact. I have learned and do follow a process of sermon development, but I am not a slave to that process.

I think a cookie-cutter approach to sermon preparation always results in a cookie-cutter sermon, and people in the pews have had enough cookies. Preaching has its do's and don'ts for sure, but even those must come under the dynamic of the Spirit, lest they become preaching legalisms that steal the life and passion from the preacher's sermon because he is so paranoid of doing a homiletic no-no. The Spirit brings life and freedom to our preaching. I think the closer my sermon reflects the text I am preaching, the more freedom and power the Spirit gives me in the pulpit. The further I get away from the Spirit-intended meaning of the text, the less power and authority the Spirit gives to my message because I am giving him less and less to witness to.

Dynamics and Mechanics Together: A Synergistic Approach

In Spirit-led preaching the *dynamics* of preaching must be viewed on equal footing with the *mechanics* of preaching. A synergistic power happens when the Word and Spirit combine. Synergism means that the sum of two combined agents is greater and more powerful than the individual elements by themselves. Therefore, Spirit-led preaching intentionally teaches preaching as a synergistic discipline—an explicit work of the Holy Spirit and the Word of God combined for the purpose of proclamation. Since the Spirit's influence drives the preaching, the Spirit-led preacher is constantly asking, "What is the Spirit's role in this aspect of the preaching process?"

Can Preaching Be Taught?

If so, who teaches us to preach? Who is qualified to teach us to preach? Some might quote 1 John 2:27, "As his anointing teaches you about all things," and take the position that the Holy Spirit is the only true teacher of preaching. Others will say that they learned to preach by watching other preachers preach or through formal training at a Bible college or seminary. Some believe you just learn it by getting up and doing it, not by reading a book about it. I believe the answer to our question is somewhere in the middle, a combination of several factors to be exact.

I believe, as a teacher of preaching, that the mechanics of sermon development can and must be learned. Many truths and principles can be taught that, combined with proper practice, can make a person a better preacher. I encourage you to keep working on your transitions. Keep working on stating the main idea of the text in a clear, pregnant, and theologically loaded sentence that your audience will never forget. Keep working on how you begin your illustrations and how you move from your last point into the conclusion.

When it comes to teaching the dynamics of preaching—the fire we must have in our bones if we are to preach with power—

the ultimate instructor is the Holy Spirit. We need to ask the hard questions about spiritual dynamics: How do you know when the Spirit speaks to you about a certain direction for your message? What is it like to experience the Spirit's empowerment while you are actually preaching? How do you know when the Holy Spirit is dealing with your congregation? How does the Spirit prompt you to put something in your message or to leave something out? Only by asking and investigating and sharing will we learn the Spirit's impact on preaching.

Learning the intangible and dynamic elements of preaching from the Holy Spirit is deeply intimate and personal. In fact, we often learn it on our knees in private prayer before the Lord. The subjective element is also present because we know the Spirit works through us individually and personally and has gifted us uniquely. This is why we cannot box the Spirit into a set formula, thereby making objective what God by design desires to be subjective. I believe the Spirit's passion manifests itself in different ways through different preachers, based on their temperaments and personalities. Jeremiah was known as the weeping prophet, yet James and John were called the Sons of Thunder! So the Spirit works in us and with us to shape the sermon through the uniqueness of our own personal walk with the Lord so that in a real sense every sermon we preach bears our own fingerprints. This is precisely why you may be able to borrow another preacher's outline, but you can never borrow his passion. This is what I mean when I say the Spirit is the teacher of the dynamic and subjective side of preaching.

Every semester I listen to students preach in our preaching labs. Some students have been pastors and have preached for a long time, but others are preaching their first sermon. Most students try to incorporate the model of mechanics that I teach them in the first semester of preaching—the central idea of the text, setting the context, keeping sermon division statements parallel and application based, and so forth. As they preach, I recognize the pattern they are following: explanation, illustration, application. In other words, all the mechanics are there, and they are following well the model they learned.

But something is missing. And by the way, you don't have to be a professor of preaching to know that something is missing; a congregation can recognize it's missing as well. What's missing is passion. The preaching lacks power, urgency, and conviction. There's no gripping intensity, no constraining burden, and no pressing compulsion. It's preaching that lacks imperative or what most people in the pew describe as "flat."

Now, when I tell a student his preaching is flat, the first question he asks is, "How do I fix it so I am not flat next time?" To begin, the way the question is asked is problematic, for it implies the pragmatism that carries the day: Just "tell me how to quick-fix this problem and I will fix it." What students eventually learn is that there is no quick fix for the dynamic element of preaching.

I tell my students: "I cannot stand over you and hold you down and make you pray. I cannot cause you to pause and pray when you see the holiness and majesty of God in the text you are studying. I cannot make your heart leap for joy at amazing grace. I cannot hold you still long enough so you can deeply and intimately come to know God (Ps. 46:10). I cannot open your eyes so that you see the wonderful things in God's Word (Ps. 119:18). I cannot put fire in your bones, or cause you to weep over your Jerusalem the way Jesus wept because of his burden for the lost and weary. Only God can do those things in you."

Preaching with conviction, passion, and urgency cannot be taught and made into a sermon step. Only when we linger long in God's presence and soak in his Word and allow his Spirit to saturate our lives can we preach under the divine imperative with conviction and power. Preach fresh from the presence of God, and you will preach with fire, and people will leave saying, "Surely the presence of the Lord was in this place today!"

The Preacher's Character: Transformation

Character matters to God. First Peter 5:3 tells us as overseers that we are to be "examples to the flock." Peter tells us, "Just as he who called you is holy, so be holy in all you do" (1 Pet. 1:15). The interrelationship between the preacher's personal life and his preaching life was captured well by Robinson, who said, "When an expositor studies his Bible, the Holy Spirit probes the preacher's life. As a man prepares sermons, God prepares the man. As the expositor masters a passage, he will discover that the truth of that passage in the hand of the Spirit masters him."[2] In other words, the man cannot be separated from the message.

Character and Proclamation

Does the spiritual condition of the preacher's life impact the message he delivers for good or for bad? Does my present walk with God impact the way I prepare and preach? Character is critical to preaching because preaching is a unique form of communication. For example, preachers cannot take the calm, cold, objective news anchor's approach to delivering the news, where the emphasis is on maintaining emotional detachment and objectivity. The "just the facts" approach may work for the daily news, but it cannot work when delivering the good news.

Nor can preachers take the approach of Broadway actors, whose main concern is to "get into the role" they are playing. Who they are in real life when the camera is turned off is of no consequence; the question is, "Can they play the role?" Can they make it credible and believable—on the stage or on the screen? In other words, the casting director does not care if the man playing a happily married husband in his production is happily married in real life. His real-life marriage could be in shambles and on the brink of another divorce, but as long as he can make the audience believe he is happily married, he is deemed successful in the eyes of the director or producer. They don't care about the actor's personal life.

In preaching, our casting director does care. Character in and out of the pulpit does matter to God. Jesus established this fact in Matthew 12:34 when he told the Pharisees, "You brood of vipers, how can you who are evil say anything good? For out of the overflow of the heart the mouth speaks." The Spirit of God is the gatekeeper of our hearts, and therefore being Spirit filled and Spirit controlled means we are bearing his fruit in our hearts (Gal. 5:22).

---

2. Haddon Robinson, "What Is Expository Preaching?" *Bibliotheca Sacra* 131 (January-March 1974): 59.

Spirit-empowered preaching is preaching out of the overflow of the heart, and that's why character counts in preaching.

Passages like Ephesians 4:26 establish this dynamic: "Do not let the sun go down while you are still angry." Unresolved anger and conflict quench the spiritual dynamic of the Christian life, so Paul warns us not to let them fester overnight—deal with them! Like leaving our offering at the altar and first reconciling with our brother, preaching demands that we are right in our relationships with others before we preach in front of others. God saves us and graciously calls us with one clear expectation for our lives: to live above reproach. In fact, when we go back and study 1 Timothy 3:2–7 concerning the qualifications of elders and overseers, we discover that God is far more concerned with our character than with our ability to preach a sermon.

This reminds us that we need to *be* who God called us to be before we *do* what God calls us to do. Preachers who desire to see God's hand on their preaching must first desire to see God's hand shape their character. The desire to preach with power must be matched with an equal desire to live holy before the Lord. The same Holy Spirit gives those two desires and empowers us to fulfill those desires. Powerful preaching comes at a price, and too few preachers today are willing to pay the price of holiness.

I once had a student begin his sermon by using an illustration from a popular crime-scene investigation television show. His text was Philippians 4:8–9, and he was referring to an episode that dealt with a murder caused by video-game violence. When he was finished, I asked him whether he had read the account in a magazine or newspaper, or whether he had viewed the show himself.

Without hesitation, he affirmed that he and his wife watched the show every week as part of their weekly viewing habits.

I followed with another question: "Do you believe that referring to a television show that is clearly in opposition to having a Philippians 4:8–9 mind undercuts your credibility or integrity as a preacher?"

"Not at all," came the reply. "I'm just trying to be relevant."

I am not going to tell you all the details of our ensuing conversation as the class came to life and began debating this issue.

What I will tell you is what really grieves my heart, even as I write this: Too many preachers today are living so close to the world that the question I asked the student *never even enters their minds.* They are comfortable in the pulpit using the world's entertainment because it has become their entertainment at home. "Is it appropriate?" has been replaced with "Is it relevant?" Preaching today is driven by the cultural connection, not the theological connection, and as a consequence we've lost the high calling and high character of preaching that the Word of God teaches.

Please don't throw down this book yet. I am not trapped in the theological ivory tower, as the last paragraph may have made you think. I do have electricity and air-conditioning at my house. I am not saying the preacher cannot or should not use media or cultural references in his preaching. Some of the most powerful sermons I have ever heard exegete the culture as well as they exegete the text. I also believe preachers need to know the culture they are trying to reach with the gospel, and they do need to preach to a twenty-first-century audience. But doing so does not require us to compromise our holiness.

My maxim is this: Make yourself aware of the culture, but don't fill yourself with the culture. You don't need to surf pornographic Web sites in order to preach a better sermon on sexual purity. You don't need to fill yourself with alcohol in order to demonstrate the devastating effects of alcoholism. As a preacher, I should be aware of what people are reading and what people are watching, but the need to be aware of something does not give me a blank check to go out and experience it firsthand.

How aware should you be of an issue? How do you become informed about something without being filled with something? Where do you draw the line? Let the holiness of God fill you, the Word of God guard you, and the Spirit of God guide you, and I think you will become less concerned with where to draw the lines and more concerned with being Christlike in your walk. Don't let the focus of your preaching pushing the edge for the sake of sensationalizing an audience. Instead, make the focus of your preaching the Word of God, and when you are in doubt about using something controversial or potentially offensive, leave it out. Paul said let the gospel offend your audience, not your sermon illustration!

Character, Preaching, and the Holy Spirit

Character and *ethos* are important because they directly influence the credibility of the messenger and the reception of the message. The Holy Spirit authenticates our message (logos) and our ethos (character) when we yield both to him, and our audience, with the Spirit's help, can discern our authenticity as preachers. Any breakdown in that dynamic severely hinders the process of communication. Character, preaching, and the Holy Spirit are all intertwined and feed off one another to produce an atmosphere of credibility and integrity. This fragile, interdependent relationship must be protected from sin and fed by a consistent devotional life filled with prayer, consecration, and meditation on God's Word for personal growth.

Failure to catch fire in the pulpit on Sunday often results from sacrificing our intimacy with God on the altar of the urgent throughout the week. Nothing is more urgent or more pressing than fanning into flame the gift God has given us (2 Tim. 1:6). Sin's aim is to put out the Spirit's fire. Sin should grieve you because it grieves the Spirit of God who lives within you. Sin should bother you because it bothers the Spirit. Righteousness should captivate your every thought because it pleases the indwelling Spirit. Purity should motivate your every decision because you are the temple of the Holy Spirit and you are not your own; you were bought at a great price.

Sin that is not confessed and repented of undermines the dynamic of the Holy Spirit and will hauntingly follow us into the pulpit and rob us of our power:

> Likewise every evasion of duty, every indulgence of self, every compromise with evil, every unworthy thought, word, or deed, will be there at the head of the pulpit stairs to meet the minister on Sunday morning, to take the light from his eye, the power from his blow, the ring from his voice, and the joy from his heart.[3]

---

3. Clarence McCartney, *Preaching without Notes* (New York: Abingdon, 1946), 176.

For example, we cannot preach Psalm 51 with a dirty heart and not feel the Spirit's conviction. We must first let the Spirit cleanse us. The Spirit won't bless a dirty life, but he will clean it. We cannot detach ourselves and preach about David's struggle as if the text applies only to David, not us. "After all," we rationalize, "our sin was not as bad as David's." But incarnational, Spirit-led preaching calls us to preach from the heart as well as from the historical. We know about David because we have studied, but we also know the weight of our own sin because of the Spirit. We know what it is like to feel the dirt of disobedience and to lose the joy of our salvation— and consequently to cry out to God for mercy and cleansing.

Only through the illumination and the empowerment of the Holy Spirit's work in our own hearts are we able to enter into the text and empathize with the Spirit's purpose in authoring the text. This "illumination" and "empowerment" are what William Still refers to as the "word becoming flesh again":

> How can a man ensure the presence and action of the Holy Spirit in his preaching? The Word must become flesh again; the preacher must become the vehicle of the Holy Spirit, and his mind inspired and his heart inflamed by the truth he preaches. This will depend not primarily on what he preaches or how he prepares, but on what he is in himself.[4]

I pray that your character will keep you where the call of God places you. Preachers sometimes let their talent take them where their character cannot keep them, and tragically they fail morally and then fall out of the ministry. Preachers are falling all around us, and I think one of the reasons is that they have not paid attention to who they are in private. Publicly they are pulpit giants, but privately because of sin they are accidents waiting to happen and time bombs waiting to go off. A lack of intimacy with God is usually the first warning sign. Then moral compromise enters because instead of depending on the Spirit, they feed the desires of the flesh. As for their preaching, they know they can get by on talent alone. They know they can pull it off

---

4. William Still, "The Holy Spirit and Preaching," *Christianity Today,* 2 September 1957, 9.

one more week. With no spiritual vitality, their preaching becomes cold and lifeless, absent of any true spiritual power. Something is missing, and before long the congregation notices it. Words may be spoken, but the Word of the Lord is not proclaimed. Failure in the pulpit almost always stems from a failure in character. Character matters to God, and it must matter to you.

Character, Sanctification, and Preaching

I believe the Bible establishes the law of sowing and reaping in Matthew 25 in the parable of the talents. The Bible teaches us that when it comes to our time, talents, and treasures, "to whom much is given, much is required." To state it another way, if we are faithful with few things, we are counted trustworthy servants, and God graciously entrusts us with more things. Luke 16:10 states: "Whoever can be trusted with very little can also be trusted with much."

According to 1 Corinthians 4, as preachers we are entrusted with the mysteries of God and are God-called stewards who must prove ourselves faithful. I believe that preaching is a trust, a sacred trust, and we are called upon to be good stewards of that trust. God honors faithfulness and therefore deepens and enriches our preaching as we faithfully respond to what he has already shown us in the Scriptures. We have been given much, and therefore God requires much of us. Consequently, a dynamic connection exists between my walk with God, my obedience to the light he has already shown me, and the depth and richness of my preaching. My progressive sanctification as a maturing Christian has a progressive and sanctifying effect on my preaching as well. The more I grow in Christ, the more my preaching grows.

The opposite is true as well: When I stagnate spiritually, my preaching stagnates. The implication is that preachers are called upon to preach out of their own sanctification. Jesus tells us to abide in him, for apart from him we can do nothing—preaching included! So our abiding in Christ, our walking in the Spirit daily, forms the foundation of Spirit-empowered preaching.

This is why we can preach the same sermon we preached two years ago and it comes out differently the second time. It's not because the material in our sermon folder has changed—the outline is the same, the exegetical notes are the same—but we are not the same. We are being sanctified as believers, and we should preach as sanctified preachers—as those whom God is continually molding and shaping through his powerful Word and his indwelling Spirit. Our sanctification is what makes us genuine and credible to the people we speak to because we are living proof (good or bad!) of what we are preaching. When we call people to come drink living water that satisfies the deepest longings of the soul, our people ought to be able to detect that we have had a drink from that fountain and that our lives are marked by its deep satisfaction.

Character and Humility

The overall goal of the Spirit at work in the heart of the preacher is one of weakness, brokenness, and absolute dependence. Paul told the Corinthians, "I came to you in weakness and fear, and with much trembling" (1 Cor. 2:3). The Spirit positions the attitude of the heart so that all glory goes to God alone. Only in our weakness do we readily acknowledge that God alone did the preaching through us. The Spirit kills our pride and our ego in order that our preaching can only be explained by the power of God.

Paul stated in 2 Corinthians 12:9 that he was brought to the point of boasting "gladly about my weaknesses, so that Christ's power may rest on me." Paul's understanding of power through weakness was derived from the fact that he knew his human depravity was only overcome by living the crucified life in the power of the Spirit. Paul's testimony in Galatians 2:20 reminds us that he was no longer the one living, but rather it was Christ who lived within him. In the same way, only crucified preachers can proclaim the crucified Savior. Remember this truth the next time you preach: You cannot make much of Jesus and much of yourself at the same time.

The call to preach as a Christ-crucified man is one of the most liberating truths you will ever embrace. When I die to self, I die to my sinful desire for popularity. When I die to self, I die to my desire to be liked. When I die to self, I no longer worry about who might get offended by the Word I am preaching. When I die to self, I quit losing sleep over an e-mail or a letter criticizing me or my message.

When I die to self, I stop worrying about whether I will get invited back again. When I die to self, I quit worrying about whether I will lose my job for calling sin what it is from the pulpit because my real employer is the King of kings and the Lord of lords, and he has plenty of work around the world to do!

When I die to self, I no longer preach "play it safe" messages that tickle ears but don't transform lives. When I die to self, I no longer feel the pressure to please a crowd or play to the audience, because a crucified preacher only preaches for an audience of one. When I die to self, I no longer rely on the latest gimmicks to keep people's attention, but I partner with the Holy Spirit and ask him to get their attention. When I die to self, I don't worry about who is going to be there while I am preaching. God is there, and that is enough.

When I die to self, I no longer feel the constant pressure to be cute, creative, or cutting edge for every new generation because the Word of God is sufficient to meet each generation where they are and take them where they need to be. When I die to self, I live as a free man in Christ, and I preach like a free man in Christ. The fear of man is replaced by the fear of the Almighty. Inhibitions give way to boldness. Reservations and hesitations fade under the radiance of preaching God's glorious Son! Spirit-led preaching is Christ-crucified preachers preaching the Christ-crucified gospel in the power of the Spirit's Christological witness. Nothing is more liberating than that.

Chapter 7

The Spirit and the Sermon's Preparation

Preaching is the art of making a sermon and delivering it. Why no, that is not preaching. Preaching is the art of making a preacher and delivering that. Preaching is the outrush of a soul in speech. Therefore, the elemental business in preaching is not with the preaching but the preacher! It is no trouble to preach—but a vast trouble to construct a preacher. What then, in light of this, is the task of the preacher? Mainly this, the amassing of a great soul as to have something worthwhile to give—the sermon is the preacher up to date.

—Ralph Turnbull

How does the Spirit get us ready to preach? That may seem like an odd question since one homiletic quip states, "Prepare like it all depends on you, and preach like it all depends on God." Although I understand the intent of such a statement, it is misleading because even in our preparation we are depending on the Holy Spirit, not ourselves. This chapter will address the Spirit's involvement in the actual preparation of the message and will focus on the elements of sermon preparation where the Spirit's influence is most clearly seen: text selection, prayer and study, sermon development, and internalizing the text.

Text Selection and the Holy Spirit

If we are going to preach Spirit-empowered sermons, we must preach *what* the Spirit wants us to preach *when* the Spirit wants us to preach it. It's that simple. Unfortunately, knowing the "what and when" can be a dreadful, draining task for those who wait all week long, hoping for the "lightbulb" to come on. On one extreme there is the great Charles Spurgeon, the prince of preachers, who candidly said to his students, "To me still, I must confess, my text selection is a very great embarrassment. . . . I confess that I frequently sit hour after hour praying and waiting for a subject, and that is the main part of my study."[1] It's hard to critique anything about Charles Spurgeon for obvious reasons, but does it have to be that difficult week in and week out? If you are a procrastinating preacher or a "week to week" specialist who does not plan ahead, perhaps Spurgeon's struggle may seem all too familiar to you. Sequential, systematic exposition might have relieved Spurgeon of the angst of his text selection every week.

On the other extreme you have preachers who plan their preaching for two years in advance and refuse to deviate from their preaching schedules even one iota. Often this planning is part of a series study or book study, where the preaching is typically verse by verse and paragraph by paragraph. This approach relieves the stress of always wondering what to preach next week, but does it allow for the Spirit to interrupt the schedule once in a while?

There must be a balance between these two extremes when it comes to selecting a text for preaching. Planning is not contrary to the Spirit, and neither are praying and waiting. The goal of our text selection is to choose the Scriptures we expound with an openness and sensitivity to the Holy Spirit and to maintain that sensitivity to the Spirit's leading for potential changes or adjustments. The Holy Spirit can lead us into a series on prayer or the family just as well as he can lead us to preach through the book of Philippians. One of the keys to Spirit-led preaching is believing you have the right message

---

1. Charles Spurgeon, *Lectures to My Students* (1893; repr., Grand Rapids: Baker Books, 1995), 84–85.

at the right time, for the right context, no matter what shape or form your preaching calendar may take.

In the first church I served as interim pastor, I prayed that the Lord would give me direction for the messages the church needed in light of their soon-arriving pastor. God directed me to the book of Colossians, in which Paul lifts up the supremacy and preeminence of Christ over all things. I believe the Spirit wanted me to challenge the church to make Christ supreme in all things, including their search for a new pastor. I was confident that the Lord led me to the book of Colossians for that specific time and for that specific church.

When the 9/11 terrorist attacks rocked our nation, many preachers changed topics and texts in order to address the shock, dismay, and insecurity many people were facing. A sermon on church discipline or financial stewardship that week would miss the significance of the moment and would miss the opportunity to address a nation in crisis. In a situation like that, changing the sermon text for the week and addressing the pain of a nation in mourning gives the congregation the sense that you are a sensitive shepherd who is listening to the Spirit. When a church member thanks you for being sensitive to the Holy Spirit, it's a compliment, not a put-down! Staying the course through the five-year study of Ezekiel because you might get behind a week shows indifference and even coldness toward the congregation.

The selection of the passage of Scripture to be preached should be driven by the Holy Spirit's leadership in the life of the preacher as he considers his congregation. Preaching occurs in the context of the church, in order to serve the church. This is why I believe the relationship a pastor has with his flock is critical to effective and powerful preaching because the shepherd must know the sheep. You don't pastor long before you can sense when your people are tired. You can sense when they are burdened with grief at consecutive deaths within the church family. You can sense when they are excited about the Lord's work or when they are challenged in their faith. The Spirit helps us discern where people are spiritually and what portion of the Word of God they need to hear from next. He is the common link between the preacher and his congregation.

The bond of love between the shepherd, his sheep, and the Spirit is essential to a healthy church. I think preaching is so rewarding and so powerful when you see the Holy Spirit using your message to speak directly to the hearts of your people. I am amazed when you follow the Spirit's leading in your preaching, and then a person on the way out the door says to you, "That's exactly what I needed this morning. It was like you were just preaching to me today!" That's the reward for being sensitive to the Holy Spirit and for boldly proclaiming the Word of God in the confidence the Spirit gives.

One of the strongest reasons for planning your preaching under the Spirit's leadership is to make sure you are providing a balanced diet of biblical exposition to your sheep. You must discipline yourself to preach the whole counsel of God. Look back over your sermons from the last five years. Do you see balance between the gospels and epistles, between narratives and wisdom literature, between Old Testament and New Testament? Sometimes by our own preferences we create our own canon within the canon and fail to show our people the richness and the fullness of God's redemptive history throughout the entire Bible.

On a side note, preachers sometimes get themselves in trouble by what I call "targeted textual preaching." The preacher has a bad week, a bad meeting, or a broken dream and in discouragement and frustration picks out a "revenge of the pastor" text for Sunday that selectively "targets" the individual or individuals who caused his pain. The Spirit never honors such preaching because its objective is getting revenge, not growing disciples. That's why preaching through a Bible book or doing a series of messages protects the preacher from wrongly using the Bible for selfish gain or revenge. Always make sure the Spirit, not your improper motives, prayerfully leads you to your text.

Studying and the Holy Spirit

The call to preach is a call to study. What the Holy Spirit illumines in the study, he will empower in the pulpit. This means we as preachers must expect the Spirit's help in the preparation of our sermon just as much as we anticipate the Spirit's help in preaching it.

Though the language is overused and clichéd, I think it is important for a preacher to be able to say with confidence, "The Lord lay this message on my heart." Spirit-led preachers who follow Spirit-directed preparation preach Spirit-empowered messages.

I prefer the language of prompting when it comes to describing the Spirit's work in the study. The Spirit prompts us internally as we read over our text, do our word studies, look up cross-references, think through applications, and develop the structure of the message. The Spirit's prompting leads us to write down certain insights we will emphasize in the delivery of our message. The Spirit may also bring to our attention something that was stored away in our hearts long ago as we prepare to preach—perhaps a story we read, an experience we had, or a verse that ministered to us at a particular time.

As I was praying about a message to preach in view of a call to be an interim pastor, I began to sense God leading me to Joshua 1. The book of Joshua begins with a leadership transition from Moses to Joshua, and the church was definitely in the midst of a time of leadership transition. As I continued to pray and study, the Spirit prompted me to talk about the doubts Israel may have experienced with their new leader Joshua: "He's not Moses, that's for sure!" It's evident from the text that Israel's new leader Joshua was fearful, for God told him over and over again in the first chapter, "Be strong and courageous!"

The message I preached was titled, "Timeless Truths for Times of Transition." I have no doubt that it was a tailor-made message for that congregation for that specific time in the life of the church. Spirit-led preaching results in tailor-made messages! After the service one lady said to me, "You know, our Moses is gone. He's not coming back. All this time I have been saying to myself, 'We'll never get another Moses,' but now I realize it's time to move on and begin preparing for our new leader."

Can I confess something? I did not want to preach that particular message at first. I was going in view of a call to this church to be their interim, and they were going to vote on me after each service that day. So in my flesh I wanted to preach a "safe" sermon, one that everyone would agree with and one that would ruffle the fewest feathers. Preach the gospel. Preach heaven. Preach love or grace or mercy. But don't get in their faces—whatever you do, don't confront them and challenge them—they may not invite you back! Had I succumbed to such a temptation, I would have been "safety led" in my preaching, not Spirit led. The Lord impressed me to preach this sermon, and to this day I believe he was testing me to see if I was truly and totally abandoned to preaching whatever he wanted, whenever he wanted it preached.

Can I challenge you to decide right now whether you are going to be Spirit led or safety led in your preaching? Are you going to tickle ears or transform lives? Are you sold out to God so much so that you will pray this prayer from your heart: "Lord, whatever you want me to say, wherever you want me to say it, whenever you want it said—I will obey you completely." Surrendering to preach means anywhere, anytime, and anything—totally at the Lord's command and discretion and totally under the Spirit's prompting and leading. That is Spirit-led preaching.

The Spirit and Laziness

A preacher cannot claim the Spirit as an excuse for laziness and a failure to do the exegetical work in a text. A preacher who ignores the work of the text is ignoring the author of the text, the Holy Spirit. The Holy Spirit will help us unpack his Word, but we have to make an effort to understand what is going on in the text. The Spirit has been abused by many preachers who simply wait for a "word from the Lord" until the last minute, rationalizing their procrastination as spirituality.

One proof text used to support the "wait and see" approach is Mark 13:11: "Whenever you are arrested and brought to trial, do not worry beforehand about what to say. Just say whatever is given you at the time, for it is not you speaking, but the Holy Spirit." The problem is that Mark 13:11 in context refers to persecuted Christians, not procrastinating preachers.

A verse that addresses sermon preparation is found in 2 Timothy 2:15: "Be diligent to present yourself approved to God, a worker who does not need to be ashamed, rightly dividing the word of truth" (NKJV). To rightly divide it means "to cut it straight," and the only way you can cut it straight is to pick it up and study it.

Notice the words *diligent* and *worker*—not exactly "wait and see" words. Spirit-led preaching actively seeks and constantly pursues the guidance, wisdom, and illumination of the Holy Spirit through prayer and then, in absolute dependence on the Holy Spirit, undertakes the hard, exegetical work of the text.

The Spirit and Illumination

Although we have previously discussed illumination in more technical detail in chapter 4, I want to come back to illumination in a more practical way in this chapter. Now that we know what illumination is, how does it operate in my weekly preparation? When we begin our times of study on our knees and we with expectant faith pray, "Open my eyes that I may see wonderful things in your law," what should we expect? Bright lights? Visions? An audible voice? No, the Spirit's illumination is not about sensational experiences that razzle and dazzle us into the spiritual ecstasy of the third heaven. The Spirit's illumination is all about our humble and obedient attitude toward the Word of God.

Illumination softens our hearts into a position of receptivity and creates expectancy in us as we anticipate the rich blessings of God's Word. Our delight in the Word is so strong and compelling that we come to the text predetermined to obey what's in it. If you want a picture of what an illumined heart looks like, read Psalm 119 and look at the verbs that underscore the relationship of the believer to God's Word: *obey, rejoice, meditate, delight, consume, direct,* and *turn.* These verbs of attitude and action come from a heart illumined by the Spirit of God.

Illumination brings us to the text with the deep conviction that God will speak to us through his text and will change our lives. When our attitude and approach to the Spirit's text are right, the illumination of the Spirit results in deep conviction as the Word of God that indelibly marks our very souls. In Spirit-led preaching the preacher prayerfully expects, seeks, welcomes, and submits to the Spirit's light given upon the text because he knows that when his heart is gripped in the study, his preaching will become gripping in the pulpit.

Warren Wiersbe shares his understanding of illumination: "I mull over the text. I pray. I meditate and exegete. I talk to my Bible, and ask questions of the text. I take notes. I think. I sweat. And then God gives me what he wants me to have."[2] The key is that the Spirit directs us and guides us into what he wants us to have. Preachers who rely solely on the sermons of others are trying to live off another preacher's illumination and are bypassing what the Spirit wants to do in their lives. We will never deliver in power what does not first reside in us with power. Praying, agonizing, repenting, thinking, changing, growing, molding, transforming, submitting, consecrating—all of these internal struggles in the study are what make for powerful preaching in the pulpit, and you cannot borrow them from somebody else.

Regardless of the words we use to describe the Spirit's work, the key to the illuminating work of the Holy Spirit is spiritual sensitivity on the part of the preacher. When our hearts are right with God, then we are ready to receive God's Word. Fundamentally, preaching is more about listening and reporting than about creating and crafting. The preacher who desires to receive the Spirit's illumination through the study of the Word of God cries out, "Speak, Lord, for your servant is listening."

Through God's Word the Spirit speaks, and he teaches us through the tense of a verb in the text how lasting and secure our salvation in Christ really is, and it blesses us. The Spirit speaks, bringing to mind a key cross-reference at just the right time in our study that sheds light on our text and lessens the ambiguity in our primary text. The Spirit speaks, piercing us with conviction about the specific application that needs to be made to our congregation. The Spirit speaks, convicting us about a specific sin in our life that we need to get right before we preach; and so we stop studying, fall to our knees, and repent. The Spirit speaks, prompting us to stop and pray for an extended period of time for the congregation's reception to what we know will be a hard but necessary truth to hear. Speak to us, Holy Spirit, through your Word, and we will listen.

---

2. E. K. Bailey and Warren Wiersbe, *Preaching in Black and White* (Grand Rapids: Zondervan, 2003), 88.

The Spirit and Shaping the Message

After all the exegetical notes from word studies and commentaries are compiled and the Spirit's illuminated insights into the text are written down, your next task is to structure and shape the message. Dependence on the Spirit at this stage is critical because you are deciding what to bring into the pulpit and what to leave in the sermon file. You are shaping and compiling the message—choosing illustrations, exegetical details, specific applications, and such. Let me begin by saying this is one of the most frustrating tasks we face as preachers because we want to bring everything we learned and studied into the pulpit; it's all good to us. Yet we know that time does not allow us to bring everything we discovered into one message. We also need to admit that we cannot empty our preaching paragraph of all that it contains in one thirty-minute sermon; this too is vanity!

So, what makes the cut? How do we know what to leave in and what to take out? Again the Holy Spirit's leadership is crucial in this element of sermon preparation. The Spirit's influence and illumination during our preparation led us to pause and ponder certain insights more than we did others; we wrote something down in bold letters with an exclamation point on our note pad; we underlined a certain phrase of the biblical text that seemed to jump off the page at us; and we highlighted a key word that the Spirit repeated three times in three verses to get our attention. As we studied, our minds were illuminated by the Holy Spirit, and we were drawn to certain words, certain verb tenses, and certain grammatical constructions. We lingered over some portions of the text longer than others because the Spirit was sharpening the focus of our sermon on a key phrase or thought. We see the Spirit-given structure of the text unfolding before our illuminated eyes, and we translate its structure into our sermon outlines.

I believe the Spirit moves and illuminates us as we carefully and contextually study his revelation, and where our minds are consumed by the biblical truth and where our hearts are compelled by the biblical truth, we should preach!

Let me give you a word of advice that I learned the hard way as a young preacher: Deliver the fruit of your study in your sermon, and spare them the details of how you went about picking it off the tree. I can remember in my early days of preaching giving exegetical overload and commentary confusion to my poor church. Serve up the juiciest and ripest fruit, and don't try to feed them the whole tree in one sermon. Remember, your exegetical sweat tends to leave the audience sour, but the fruit of your labor tastes sweet as the Spirit takes it and produces more fruit in the believer's life. May this be the prayer of your own heart: "Holy Spirit, help me to know what to include and what to emphasize in this message I'm preparing. I'm depending on you to give me wisdom as I pull this message together and preach it so that what I take into the pulpit and deliver accurately reflects your Word and is precisely what you want me to say and deliver."

The Spirit and Incarnational Preaching

Having experienced the Spirit's leadership in putting the message together, we now cast ourselves upon the Holy Spirit to internalize and incarnate the truth we are going to preach. The good news is that the Holy Spirit has been helping us to do this throughout our lives, and therefore the process of internalization is cumulative. We internalize God's Word when we know it and apply it to our lives so that its impact stays with us. It is more than memorizing a verse for Sunday morning's sermon; it is letting the Spirit rub the Scriptures deep into our lives.

Some preachers I know quit before they internalize the message. "I have my outline" or "I have my manuscript" is paramount to quitting time in the study. But a sermon is more than delivering an outline or delivering a manuscript; it's about incarnating the truth and delivering your soul through your sermon. Here's a question for you: if you lost your sermon outline or manuscript, could you still preach your message? If your message is incarnated in your heart, you can!

Defining Incarnational Preaching

The concept of incarnational preaching was perhaps best expressed by Philip Brooks in his classic definition of preaching:

Truth through personality is our description of real preaching. The truth must come really through the person, not merely over his lips, not merely into his understanding and out through his pen. It must come through his character, his affections, his whole intellectual and moral being. It must come genuinely through him.[3]

The biblical basis for incarnational preaching is the earthly incarnation of Jesus Christ. John's Gospel states, "The Word became flesh and made his dwelling among us. We have seen his glory, the glory of the One and Only, who came from the Father, full of grace and truth" (John 1:14). As Christ the Word became incarnate flesh, the preacher also should incarnate God's revealed Word by the Spirit's power. The result is a preacher who visibly manifests "grace and truth" in the pulpit. In Spirit-led preaching, incarnating the message we preach is critical to the Spirit's purpose of transformation. What people need to see in the pulpit is someone who has been changed and transformed by the truth he is proclaiming, not an imposter under the pretense of false spirituality.

As a preacher, you are an incarnate testimony of what your text is saying. People in the audience can see that you have been with Jonah in the belly of the great fish. They can smell the decaying body of Lazarus as you preach Jesus, the resurrection and the life. They hear the screams of the demoniac as you paint the picture of unceasing torment in the text. They taste the anguish of the Passover meal that Jesus shared with his disciples. It's not so much that you transport your audience back to Mary and Martha's first-century house but rather that you visit in their house long enough so that your audience senses you have been there yourself.

Keys to Internalizing the Message

What are the keys to internalizing the message? How can a preacher more effectively incarnate the truth he will preach? First, the preacher must be committed to prayer. I think praying your sermon back to God as an offering of worship is a powerful way to

---

3. Phillips Brooks, *Lectures on Preaching* (New York: E. P. Dutton, 1898), 8.

keep your preaching in the context of worship and to remind yourself who you are preaching for. Ask God to burn the truth on your heart first so you can deliver it hot to others. Follow the wisdom of sermon preparation that goes, "Read yourself full, think yourself clear, pray yourself hot, and deliver yourself empty."

Second, the preacher must take time to internalize. You must allow time for the message to germinate in your heart, soul, and mind. Preaching requires an incubation period for full development to take place. To finalize your sermon preparation by finishing point three of your message while the choir is singing on Sunday morning is cutting it a little too close for comfort! Soak yourself in the text, and give it time to soak into you. Time away from the intensity of preparation can also provide moments of insight as well because the Spirit never ceases to give us guidance in understanding and communicating truth. That's why you keep a pad and pen handy in your car or in your pocket, or even beside your bed, because here's what happens. When you internalize your message, you constantly are turning it over in your mind. You go for a walk or for a run, and it hits you—a way into the text, your conclusion, the perfect illustration, a penetrating application. The Spirit honors your persistent thinking and wrestling with the text.

Third, for incarnational preaching to take place, there must be a fresh commitment to clear thinking. Just as food needs time to digest in order to become useful to the body, so the preacher needs time not just to unearth the truth of a particular passage, but to think about it and digest its significance and implications. Like an Olympic downhill skier who visualizes every inch of the course before the gate is even opened, so the preacher needs to think through the sermon from start to finish, visualizing how he will negotiate every segment. Transitions, illustrations, explanations, and applications should be clearly thought out. Most of us make time to read, to translate, to write, and to study; but do we plan times to think and meditate on the flow and path our sermon will take?

The fourth key to incarnational preaching is the preacher's resolution to be himself in the pulpit. Everyone has a preconceived idea or image of what a preacher is supposed to look like and how a preacher should act. The preacher who tries to become all preachers to all people fails because the Spirit has uniquely shaped you and transformed you to be who you are, not someone else. One of the surest ways a preacher can hinder the work of the Holy Spirit is trying to impress people by acting like someone other than who God created him to be. Don't try to force yourself into a mold that the Spirit did not ask you to fill. In Spirit-led preaching, the incarnational emphasis demands that we genuinely and authentically live out the Spirit's work in our own hearts and lives. People can spot a fake, bottom line. Any hint of showmanship or imitation quenches the work of the Spirit. The only safeguard to these temptations is for the preacher to embrace wholeheartedly his calling from God to be God's own unique man.

I want to end this chapter with an illustration that I think will help you get a handle on the Spirit's involvement in sermon preparation. My wife is a great cook. She makes some great meals using many different methods of cooking, but my favorites tend to come out of the Crock-Pot. I love the food that comes out of the Crock-Pot, but I do not love the time it takes to prepare it. "Can't you just stick it in the microwave?" I ask. "No, it will not taste the same," she replies.

Powerful, Word-saturated, and Spirit-filled preaching comes from the Crock-Pot, not the microwave. Preachers who try to microwave God's truth on the "quick and easy" setting in the name of "saving time" will find that the meal from God's Word will not taste the same. Spirit-led preaching calls for the slow-simmering effect of the Crock-Pot, where the longer the meal saturates in the simmering heat of the Crock-Pot, the juicier and more tender it becomes. How are you preparing and serving God's Word each week: microwave or Crock-Pot?

Chapter 8

The Spirit and the
Sermon's Presentation

*A close link between the preacher and the Holy
Spirit must be maintained for effective preaching.
The Spirit is the energizer, the dynamite of powerful
preaching. We need the unction, the anointing of the
Holy Spirit, lest our words, eloquent or otherwise,
bounce off recalcitrant hearts and evaporate. Ours is
a commitment to the Word and Spirit. The Spirit comes
through the Word and with the Word, but not apart from
or without the Word.*

—R. C. Sproul

Perhaps the most common misconception about the Holy Spirit
and preaching is the belief that the Holy Spirit shows up only
when the sermon is preached. After all, not many church
members who were touched by the sermon say to us on the way out
the door, "The Spirit was really moving in your office today." Instead
they say, "The Spirit was moving in church today through your
message." They locate the Spirit's power in the sanctuary, not the
study. As preachers, we know the Spirit has been involved all along,
preparing us to deliver God's Word. We experience his illumination
in the study, and we anticipate his empowerment in the pulpit.

When it comes to sermon delivery, is there a style of delivery
that works best with the Holy Spirit's ministries for preaching? Can

101

we follow our notes and follow the Spirit at the same time? What is the link between the preacher, the text, and the congregation? These and other questions will fill this chapter as we examine the Spirit's role in presenting the message.

The Preacher and Delivery

The "dilemma of delivery," as Vines calls it, is beyond the scope of this book. Rather than defining and debating the different approaches to sermon delivery, this chapter seeks the answer to a narrower question: "What method of sermon delivery best fits Spirit-led preaching?" Some preachers think that the Spirit isn't even interested in our delivery; they stand to preach, open their mouths, the Spirit takes over, and the rest doesn't matter. Others think that minimizing notes and being extemporaneous in delivery gives preachers more freedom to follow the Spirit into the unplanned elements of the sermon.

Regardless of delivery style, almost all preachers agree that there are times when they have preached when they have been more keenly aware of the Spirit than at other times. There are also moments when the Spirit's empowering presence shows up in a way that surprises them because they were not as prayed up and prepared as they should have been. Consequently, the bottom line of this chapter may be this: the sovereign Spirit of God works with a variety of delivery styles and uses those styles to proclaim his truth through us. Passionate, engaging delivery that remains open to the Spirit's extemporaneous leadership is ideal.

We want to avoid distracting delivery that takes attention away from the Word and focuses it on the messenger. So we pray and ask the Holy Spirit to help us preach in a way that will not hinder his work. We refine our delivery skills so that our distracting movements, darting eyes, or monotone voice does not distract the listener. Poor delivery skills draw attention to the speaker, not the message. In fact, the preachers with the best delivery skills often go unnoticed in their delivery, as they should. What does get noticed is their message, and that's what matters.

Rarely will a preacher hear a church member or visitor say, "You've got the greatest delivery skills I have ever seen on planet

Earth; you are a total package!" But if your delivery skills are bad and you cannot make it through a sermon without at least three 327 fillers—uhms and uhs—then you can be sure your poor delivery skills will put the spotlight on you, not your message. Hearing God's Word becomes more difficult because listeners are trying to work around your poor delivery of the message.

I know the Spirit of God can use us in spite of ourselves and all our inadequcies, but that's no excuse for not working on our delivery deficiencies. Remember, we preach for God's glory. If anything in our delivery takes away from his glory, then we need to change it—period!

Delivery and Style

One of the first and most obvious choices for sermon delivery is the use of extensive notes or even a full manuscript. Manuscript preaching typically limits the preacher to the pulpit and ties the preacher closely to his printed notes. Movement and eye contact still can happen, though often on a more limited basis. The question is whether the preacher can remain open and sensitive to the Holy Spirit while using notes. A preacher who uses extensive notes or a manuscript and who determines in his mind not to depart one iota from what he has written can hardly be interacting with his audience, much less the Spirit. If a preacher can maintain an openness and freedom to the Spirit's influence and engage the audience while using notes, then he should consider using them. By openness I mean willingness to allow the Spirit to edit our message in the heat of our delivery, even to take our sermon in a different direction. Though this may be a rare occurrence for some and a frequent occurrence for others, we all must remain submissive and open to the "Spirit of all truth."

For some, preaching from notes or a manuscript is more of a hindrance than a help. The written material becomes like a "ball and chain," and the preacher spends more time preoccupied with the manuscript than with the audience. I call these "stop and go" preachers. They go for a minute, they stop to find their place in their notes, gather their thoughts, and then they go for another minute or two before they repeat the process. Like someone learning to drive a stick shift, stop-and-go preaching loses the audience because the preaching loses its flow.

Now before you go patting yourself on the back because you don't preach with notes, let me say that using notes can be done effectively; and some of the most powerful, Spirit-filled preachers I have heard use notes and use them well. The issue is not one of method but of skill. Seasoned preachers who use extensive notes or even manuscripts know how to mark their notes and manuscripts effectively so that when they look down their eyes quickly catch the thought and they continue. Rarely do they lose their place, and rarely do they break eye contact for long. Glancing down to get a thought is not the same as reading word for word. When they need to read a quote, they read it well, with energy and passion.

Also, the best preachers who use notes maintain fairly good eye contact and typically do not give their audiences the impression they are enslaved to their manuscripts or notes. What they have to say is so engaging and thought provoking that the use of notes becomes a nonissue. What they may lack in style, they make up for in substance.

Another approach to delivery is the memorized message. Instead of the preacher relying on his notes for recall, he commits the entire message, or at least large portions of it, to memory. This puts a great pressure on the preacher that I believe can be counterproductive to remaining open to the Spirit's guidance. Memorization consumes a great deal of time and tends to put the preacher's focus on not forgetting something. The preacher's preoccupation with the fear of losing his place in the message quenches his openness to the Spirit.

One approach that helps the preacher focus on the dynamic of the Holy Spirit is the incarnational model of preaching discussed in the previous chapter. If a message has been internalized, then what happens in delivery is essentially preaching from the overflow of internalization. When a message is properly internalized, delivery embodies the message of the text. Our people recognize the congruence between our subject matter and our expression of it through delivery.

When we preach the beginning of Psalm 51, we are crushed and broken like David as we begin, not smiling and lighthearted. When we seek cleansing and ask for restoration, hope begins to enter our voices, and our body language shows signs of expectancy because all is not lost. Then we hit the high point of verse 15: "Open my lips, and my mouth will declare your praise." Our delivery at this point in the text embodies celebration and rejoicing, for David is ready to worship, having been made clean. We are ready to worship with him, for we know what it's like for sin to steal our worship, but we also know the sheer joy of praising God with clean hands and a pure heart.

Incarnational preaching calls the preacher to allow the truth he proclaims to flow through his personality so that gestures, facial expressions, eye communication, and vocal dynamics reflect the truth of the text and the Spirit's movement in the preacher's life. The result is natural, genuine, and authentic delivery that emphasizes openness and sensitivity to the Spirit's leading.

For some preachers the incarnational model of delivery can take place while using notes. Instead of being a slave to the notes, the preacher trusts the Spirit to take him beyond his notes and in an extemporaneous fashion authentically reflect the meaning in the message. On the other hand, we do not discount all the work the Spirit did in our preparation and suddenly set aside our notes and seek a fresh word from the Spirit right before we speak. If you followed the Spirit's illumination of the text in the study, you will be plenty fresh come time to preach!

Nor do we go to the other extreme and totally block the Spirit from our presentation, fearing he might move us off our notes and into unknown and uncharted territory. Instead, we need to experience the Spirit's liberty and freedom while we preach by remaining faithful to the text and open to the Spirit's dynamic taking shape between us and our audience. If the Spirit's message is in our hearts, then let the Word that is in us become flesh and dwell among our listeners.

Whether they preach using notes or without notes, Spirit-led preachers agree on one thing: they trust the Holy Spirit to empower their delivery of the message. In many ways preaching is an act of faith that calls us to trust God as we follow through on his divine call on our lives to speak his truth. As preachers, we believe and trust that the Spirit of God who has called us will stand beside us and help us execute our divine mandate as we deliver the message he has birthed in our hearts and minds. We depend on the Holy Spirit to fill us, to control us, to stand beside us, and to preach through us: "But the Lord stood at my side and gave me strength, so that through me the message might be fully proclaimed and all the Gentiles might hear it" (2 Tim. 4:17).

Delivery and Indeterminacy

The need for a method of sermon delivery with freedom and openness to the Spirit is grounded in the belief in what homileticians call sermonic indeterminacy. Indeterminacy is the idea that a sermon is not really a sermon until it is preached before the audience in "real time." What scholars call "indeterminacy," I like to call the "wild-card factor" of preaching. The wild-card factor is the unpredictable element of preaching that you can only discern and engage extemporaneously; no amount of planning or preparation will help.

Some wild-card factors: you arrive and there is no pulpit, so you preach from the floor, and you notice how much more intimate the setting becomes. The microphone stops working, and you find yourself straining vocally. The testimony goes longer than you anticipated, and you have to decide whether to preach everything you had planned, preach half of what you planned, or just head straight to the invitation. During the solo you decide to start the sermon in a different way because of the lyrics of the song that was just sung. You were going to use an illustration from *Sponge Bob Square Pants,* but then you notice a petition on the church foyer wall that reads, "Contact the FCC to Squash Square Pants." (OK, I threw that one in there to see if you were awake.)

So we plan, prepare, pray, and present; but we are always open and ready to follow the Spirit's lead as we discern each unique occasion.

Indeterminacy also means that as preachers we must expect the Spirit to move in real time. We pay attention to our audience. We mingle with them before the sermon and get a feel for what is on their hearts and minds. We adjust, we adapt, and we let the Spirit contextualize us and our message for the specific occasion. Sermonic indeterminacy is one reason some preachers do not believe in recording or videotaping the service. Their conviction is that the sermon is a sermon when it is preached in real time—period. Any CD or DVD can never capture the interactive dynamics of the audience or the preacher.

Let me illustrate the "sermon is not a sermon until it is preached" phenomenon. One of the experiences God has blessed me with is being able to serve as an interim pastor. This church has multiple services on Sunday—9:15 a.m. and 11:00 a.m. and 6:00 p.m. I prepare and preach the same message at all three services, but the services never turn out to be the same. At first this frustrated me a little because the messages were never identical in any of the services. The math just doesn't add up; same text + same outline + same PowerPoint slides + same preacher = different messages with different outcomes.

Then I realized what was happening: I was experiencing sermonic indeterminacy. One week the 9:15 crowd was awake and electrified. I fed off their energy and enthusiasm and responded by preaching eight minutes longer than I did in the second service—adding some "unplanned" elements that were birthed in the moment of interaction between preacher and congregation. Unprompted applause and amens will do that to a preacher.

Then 11:00 came. There was a lethargy and heaviness over the audience compared to the excited energy of the 9:15 service. Same message, but a different crowd dynamic this time produced a more subdued delivery. Was I fatigued? Was I out of homiletic gas already? Or was it because the audience is a little older and more reserved at the 11:00 service? The crazy thing about indeterminacy is that the next week the situation was reversed; 9:15 was still sleepy, and 11:00 was on fire! Go figure.

So in a real sense the preacher who is open to the Spirit's leading and sensitive to the dynamic of indeterminacy must learn to work with what the audience or the context gives him. By the way, because I believe in sermonic indeterminacy and because I do not believe my sermon is inerrant, I change and edit my sermon between services. I cut the introduction back because it was too long and too detailed. I add an illustration that answers the question that was raised in a conversation I was having between services. I put a new note in my Bible because I forgot to mention in the first service the verse where Jesus declared all foods to be clean.

Now back to the evening service. At the six o'clock service, the worship is full-blown contemporary. My suit and tie from the morning are gone, replaced by much more casual dress and a much more casual atmosphere. The vertical nature of the worship also makes the atmosphere more contemplative; a holy seriousness pervades the room. Hands are raised, eyes are closed, and the music addresses God directly.

So my preaching style adapts to my environment. I use the same text from the same sermon series in the morning, but my preaching becomes more reflective and introspective. I ask more probing questions. The pace is slower to match the audience. I find that my dramatic pauses are more prominent. I drop my opening humor from the morning so I do not break the holy seriousness created by the last worship song. My message is a bit longer at night because I sense people are with me, sitting up, taking notes, and making meaningful eye contact with me. They are not in a hurry to get out and head for lunch.

One person who came to a morning and evening service on the same Sunday told me, "You preach a little differently at night than you do in the morning." That's indeterminacy! That's sensitivity to the context in which you are preaching. That's Spirit-led preaching.

Delivery and Openness

What exactly is openness to the Spirit in delivery? I believe it means that you are listening to the Spirit's voice while you preach and trusting his leadership to guide you through the message he has placed on your heart. Through prayerful dependence, we demonstrate that preaching is the Spirit's ministry, not ours. In our surrendered state the Holy Spirit as the author of our message is also free to serve as editor in chief as we deliver the message. In a practical sense, openness to the Spirit means you may change a word or use a different thought to explain something. Openness to the Spirit may mean you leave out an illustration that pops into your head because the Spirit immediately gives you an uneasiness about using it so you pass on it. Perhaps you apply a biblical truth in a different way than you had previously planned. Openness to the Spirit means you quote a verse you had not planned on quoting because the Spirit brings it to your remembrance because you previously had hid it in your heart. The verse never may have made it into your notes; but in the moment of delivery, the Spirit brings it to mind; and after you finish preaching, someone says it was just the verse they needed to hear. Spurgeon agrees that there is a sense of indeterminacy in preaching:

> I do not see where the opportunity is given to the Spirit of God to help us in preaching, if every jot and tittle is settled beforehand. Do let your trust in God be free to move hand and foot. While you are preaching, believe that God the Holy Spirit can give you, in the same self-hour, what you shall speak; and can make you say what you had not previously thought of; yes, and make this newly-given utterance to be the very arrowhead of the discourse, which shall strike deeper into the heart than anything you had prepared.[1]

A word of caution is in order regarding the Holy Spirit's prompting: not everything that pops into your mind while you are preaching is always the Spirit's work. We are illumined but not inspired when we preach. Preachers are human and can say wrong things, careless things, and even hurtful things. We need the Spirit's restraining work as much as we need his illuminating work. Openness to the spontaneity of the Spirit must also include submission to his restraint. If the preacher genuinely prays, "Lord, may everything that comes from my mouth this day be pleasing in your sight," then he should expect and trust the Holy Spirit to strain out all extraneous material as well as anything that might be derogatory and later regrettable.

In my own preaching, there have been many times in the middle of my sermons where I wanted to say something that flashed into my mind; but instead of saying it right away, I took a long pause and after a few moments of reflection decided to move on and leave

---

1. Charles Spurgeon, *An All-Around Ministry* (Carlisle, Pa.: Banner of Truth, 1995), 349–50.

it unsaid. The congregation thinks it is a planned dramatic pause of some sorts, but in reality I am searching my own heart and allowing the Holy Spirit to check my motives and my attitude for wanting to include it. If the Spirit can lead us to put it into the sermon, he can also lead us to leave it out of the sermon.

Delivery and Passion

Where does passion come from? Why do people who listen to preaching continually list passion as one of the key factors they look for in an effective message? I believe listeners identify with passion because passion is contagious. Aristotle referred to a speaker's passion as pathos—meaning the speaker was gripped and transformed by what he was saying. As for its origin, the Spirit of God births passion in our hearts long before we stand to preach on Sunday. If you're not passionate about your message before Sunday at 11:00, no amount of psyching yourself up will help; it's too late for genuine, heartfelt passion.

You can mark your sermon notes with a Post-It Note that says, "Get passionate at this point," but it won't help because passion is not planned; it is incarnated. You can yell and sweat and wave a hanky, but folks will see right through your bogus attempt to work the crowd into a frenzy. True passion is not contrived or coerced; instead it is birthed from the power of the Word of God and the conviction of the Holy Spirit. Passion is not a light switch we can turn on or off at will; rather, passion erupts out of an ever-growing, ever-vital, and ever-dynamic relationship with Jesus Christ, the Word of God, and the Holy Spirit. When we are convinced that we are preaching the living, active, and powerful Word of God, we come under the Spirit's conviction and like Jeremiah express passion because we have fire in our bones.

Delivery and Connecting

Ask preachers today how to connect with an audience, and you will find a million different answers. "Know their culture." "Live in their world." "Be real." "Speak their language." "Listen to their music." "Be authentic." Not many mention the work of the Holy Spirit, which goes to show how culturally driven preaching has become these days. Theologically driven preaching relies on the Word of God preached in the power of the Holy Spirit to make the connection with the audience. The Word's efficacy is grounded in Isaiah 55:11 (NKJV): "My word . . . shall not return to Me void, but it shall accomplish what I please." The Spirit's efficacy is John 16:13: "But when he, the Spirit of truth, comes, he will guide you into all truth." Together they make a powerful team that can exegete the passage as well as the audience.

The Spirit's involvement in preaching does not negate the preacher's knowing something about the culture of his audience. Jesus knew the farming culture of Palestine would relate to agricultural stories so he talked about seeds, barns, and soils. Spurgeon said we should preach with the Bible in one hand and the newspaper in the other (Web sites and blogs would better fit our culture today). What Spirit-led preaching does not advocate is thinking that the knowledge of culture is the way into a person's heart. Knowing the culture may help us gain a hearing, but it can never open the heart. Like Lydia in Acts 16, only the Holy Spirit can open the heart; and he opens it through the truth of the Word, not because we can connect well with an audience.

If the Spirit of God and the Word of God help us connect with our audience in a supernatural sense, what is the preacher's role? How do we connect with our audiences when we deliver the message? First of all, in order to connect with the audience in an authentic and engaging manner, the preacher's delivery should acknowledge the audience in the first place. Have we not all experienced messages where the preacher seemed so absorbed in his notes and in what he was doing that he was oblivious to what was going on in the audience? Some preach like there's no audience present.

Once I was asked to make a video for a church that was considering me to be their next pastor. I had sent them audio cassettes of messages I had preached, but I did not have a video I was willing to send them. I hope you noticed the strategic use of the word *willing* in that last sentence. It was not that I did not have a video. I had a few, but remember I was trying to impress this pastor search team, not depress them with one of my classroom preaching videos. Some of you are smiling right now because you have some videos of yourself preaching that you will never let anybody see. You yourself saw it once, but that was enough—never again! Keep your old sermons around to encourage you when you get fed up with your current preaching because popping in a videotape or DVD gives you an instant reason to rejoice: I am not where I ought to be in my preaching, but praise God I am not where I used to be! Can I get a witness?

Being rather desperate to get this church a video, I went to my preaching lab at the seminary after hours and preached a sermon I had been working on. I put the tape in, hit *record,* ran to the pulpit, and started preaching. A few weeks later I got an e-mail from the search team, asking me if I had preached the sermon before an audience. Busted! They could tell I was in an artificial environment. They could tell I had no audience to interact with. Had I been thinking, I should have at least paid some students to come in and say "Amen!" during the sermon.

The problem with my delivery in that artificial environment was just that; it was artificial. That search team could tell I was in "dress rehearsal" mode and was going through the motions. Churches are looking for preachers who engage and interact with their audience when they preach.

Delivery and Prayer

Is it hypocritical for our prayer life to intensify right before we preach? If we pray with more intensity because we understand the eternal significance (1) of what is at stake when we preach or (2) of what we are doing when we stand to preach, then I think we are praying without false pretense. But if our prayer life suddenly kicks into high gear because it's Saturday night or Sunday morning and we have nothing to say because we have not prepared, then I do think it's hypocritical suddenly to become very prayerful.

What preacher has not felt the angst of 11:00 Sunday approaching, waking up, looking back over the message, and thinking, *Lord, this sermon is going to be so weak and powerless without you! I am so inadequate, so weak, so I call on you to strengthen and uphold me as I stand today and proclaim your Word.* Preachers don't preach long before they know the importance of getting their hearts right with God before they preach. Preach one sermon when your heart is not right before the Lord, and you will do everything in your power never to let it happen again. It's one of the worse feelings and experiences in the world. When you preach dirty from harboring sin in your heart, you feel naked, alone, and spiritually flat like someone who has been abandoned. So we must pray before we preach and even while we are preaching.

Spurgeon attributed his pulpit power to the fact that people were praying for him while he was preaching. I wonder who prays for you while you are preaching? Prayer humbles us before a holy God as we beg and plead for him to take the gifts of the Spirit and the Word and bless the church. Our own words spoken in our own strength are empty; but God's Word, spoken from our anointed lips, is life! Ask the Spirit of God to fill you and empower you as you preach, and ask the Lord to anoint you as his servant of the Word. Let me share with you a prayer that I wrote to help prepare my own heart right before I preach.

A Preacher's Prayer

O God, break me just now; I feel pride in my heart. God forgive me, for I find myself more consumed with thoughts of how well I will do rather than trusting completely in what you alone can do. I repent of all prideful thoughts and impure motives that place the focus today on my own glory rather than your glory. Kill within me that part of me that pressures me to perform and do well when I preach because I have a desire to be liked, a reputation to uphold, or a title before my name to fulfill. Help me preach like a man who has been crucified with Christ so that the sheep see that it is not I but Christ who lives within me preaching today. Remind me constantly today that I am a sinner saved by grace—no more, no less.

O God, teach me afresh what it means to die to self—even in a pulpit! Remind me again today that preaching your Word is a gift and a grace. I did nothing to earn it, and I've done nothing to deserve it. Indeed, I am not worthy to proclaim the riches of your glory. As you humbled Isaiah in his day, humble me before I preach, before your throne of glory. As I prepare to step behind the pulpit today and break the bread of life, remind me that I am called to this family of faith to serve bread to your hungry people. Give me a love for my flock, and make me a blessing to them today. As your herald, help me to proclaim with boldness the truth. Remind me even now that I am not in this to make a name for myself; I am in this to make much of Jesus.

O God, save souls today as I lift up Jesus before the eyes of the lost. Burden me even now with their eternal state. Empty me now of all the vain things that charm me most; I sacrifice them to his blood. Fill me with the Holy Spirit, and empower me to preach your Word with conviction and power. And when the message is over and the people begin to leave, I pray none would leave saying, "What a great preacher we heard today." Instead, I pray that all will leave in awe of you, saying, "What a mighty God we serve!"

Preaching as Trialogue:
The Spirit, the Preacher, and the Congregation

The next section of this chapter on the presentation of the message will focus on the receiving end of the communication process, the audience. Some preachers pay little attention to the audience because they view preaching as a monologue on Sunday that is the result of a dialogue they had with the Lord in their study all week long. Others see preaching as a dialogue between the preacher and the audience, and they unknowingly leave the Holy Spirit out of the conversation. I think we need a fresh approach to this area of preaching, and therefore I propose that instead of thinking of preaching as monologue or dialogue, we coin a new phrase that reminds us of the Spirit's presence and contribution as well: trialogue.

Preaching as trialogue means the presentation of the message becomes a three-way conversation between the preacher, the audience, and the Holy Spirit. What are they all talking about? The Word of God! Preaching as trialogue reminds us of the dynamic and interactive element of preaching because preaching does not happen in a vacuum. The Spirit's desire is not to take a backseat and simply "overhear" or "oversee" the preacher-audience conversation. The Spirit wants to contribute actively and directly to the trialogue by quickening the hearts and minds of the audience to hear and respond to the Word and by empowering and guiding the preacher's presentation of the Word of God.

Spirit-led preaching as a trialogue emphasizes the fact that the Spirit, the preacher, and the audience are meeting together to hear and experience the Word of God together. Powerful preaching comes through the dynamic interaction of the three entities: (1) The preacher proclaims the Word in the power of the Holy Spirit. (2) The Spirit gives his *testimonium* to the Word being preached. (3) The audience resounds with "Amen, it's true!" as they yield to the Spirit's inward application of the proclaimed Word of God to their own hearts.

If one of the participants in the trialogue does not show up and contribute, then true transformational preaching doesn't happen. If the preacher ignores the audience and focuses only on his manuscript, a monologue takes place. If the preacher and audience fail to invite the Spirit into the presentation and reception of God's Word, a dialogue takes place. If the preacher comes to the conversation unprepared because of lack of study, he will have nothing to contribute to the conversation. If the audience comes to hear God's Word with a carnal mind and a sin-filled heart, they will not be able to contribute to the conversation. If the Spirit is ignored by the audience and the preacher, then the preaching will be talk but not transformation. Only in the trialogue—where the Spirit, the preacher, and the audience are all engaged in a three-way transformational convergence centered on the Word of God—does powerful preaching take place.

The Spirit and the Congregation

In Spirit-led preaching, the congregation plays a critical role in the task of preaching. From the very beginning the congregation or audience is by design factored into the sermon. Going back to our working definition of preaching, remember that our preaching is always done "with a view to applying the text by means of the convicting power of the Holy Spirit, first to the preacher's own heart, and then to the hearts of those who hear, resulting in Spirit-filled living and a demonstration of the Spirit's power." The preacher who gives no prayerful thought to the "hearts of those who hear" will find those hearts coldly closed when he stands to preach. If he has no burden for them in the study, he will have no burden for them in the pulpit.

Instead, Spirit-led preachers meet their audience on their knees, as they pray that their listeners will combine the proclaimed Word of God with Spirit-enabling faith. "For we also have had the gospel preached to us, just as they did; but the message they heard was of no value to them, because those who heard did not combine it with faith" (Heb. 4:2).

In Spirit-led preaching, the Spirit's desired response from the audience must be at the forefront of the preacher's mind throughout the preparation and planning of the sermon. We plan, we pray, we choose our illustrations, and we make our specific applications under the Spirit's direction and with the congregation in mind. Instead of taking the vague, irresponsible, and haphazard approach of "just preach the Bible and let the Spirit of God sort it all out later," the Spirit-led preacher intentionally trusts the Spirit to accompany his message and escort it into the hearts of the audience for their digestive transformation.

We preach with a deep trust in the fact that only the Holy Spirit changes minds and opens hearts. This is why partnering with the Holy Spirit for preaching is liberating, because preachers don't have to resort to arm-twisting, guilt-tripping, and manipulating shenanigans.

The Congregation and Expectancy

In a perfect world every member of your church would come to God's house full of the Holy Spirit and full of the Word of God. They study the passage with you all week long in the original languages as they sit around the dinner table each night. They pray unceasingly for you, for the message, and for their own receptivity to your message. They sleep ten hours before coming to church on Sunday and walk in rested and refreshed. They will not fall asleep on you—ever (perfect world, remember). They fast all week, but on Sundays they have a nutritious breakfast right before church so they will be full of energy. They do not fight with their spouses on the way to church, nor do they argue with their kids about driving the car home after church. They arrive early and are never late. They quietly meditate in the sanctuary as they wait in expectancy for the service to start, eagerly anticipating the spiritual meal you have prepared for them from God's Word.

Unfortunately, we have to wake up from this "perfect world" now and realize that most congregations are poorly prepared to hear the Word of God and that they come with minimal expectations when they come to hear us preach. I know there are rare exceptions, and you should thank God if you happen to preach to an exceptional audience. The reality we face each week is daunting. People come physically tired, emotionally drained, and preoccupied with the work that is waiting on their desk tomorrow. They are distracted by the full day they have planned ahead, including lunch, the big game or race, cutting the grass, washing the car, and other things. They got up late, argued on the way to church, got upset because they couldn't find a close parking space, and then came into church after the service started only to find some visitor had their seat! Now do you think they are ready to combine the Word with faith?

If we supplement this scenario with current cultural studies, then on top of this scenario we would also add the fact that people's attention spans are getting shorter and shorter, so we need to move to a more sound-bite approach to preaching that takes small commercial breaks in between sermon points. We are told this generation is visual, not aural, so quit trying to make them listen to sermons and play them something they can look at on the big screen. They don't know the Bible, so why do you keep using it every week? And they don't like propositional truth, either, but they can tolerate your stories in moderation.

If you think your creativity and ingenuity can reach that kind of audience week in and week out on a consistent basis, then you don't need the Holy Spirit because you are the Holy Spirit! If the weight of breaking through such dismal and depressing circumstances each week was all on our shoulders, we would have given up by now for something much less intimidating. God knows what we are up against in preaching, and he knows it cannot be done in our own strength, with our own skills, and with our own creativity. I will go ahead and apologize in advance if I bruise your ego with this next statement, but the bottom line is this: none of us is that good at preaching!

I ask again, "What is a preacher to do in these days?" Partner with the Holy Spirit and trust him to prove faithful to preaching so that he manifests himself as the true communicator who can overcome any obstacle that stands in the way of hearing the Word of God. With the Spirit's aid, we can overcome every barrier that stands in the way.

The Congregation's Responsibility

The Spirit-dependent preacher trusts the Holy Spirit to empower the message, but does the church? The preacher knows he must be Spirit filled while preparing and presenting the message, but do the hearers know they must be Spirit filled in order properly to receive the message? One of the responsibilities Spirit-led preachers must accept is training and teaching the church about preparing to receive and obey God's Word. You have a God-given calling to feed the flock, but before they can eat what you serve them, they need to learn how to wash up before they dig in and eat. They need to learn how to chew their food, how to digest it, so as to maximize its effectiveness for spiritual transformation.

What are the responsibilities given to the congregation for the preaching of the Word? First of all, we must teach the flock who the Spirit is and what they can expect him to do in their lives. Let me encourage you to do a series of messages on the Holy Spirit and take them through John 14–16. Study the Spirit's role in evangelism in the book of Acts. Build within them a biblical theology of the Holy Spirit. Teach them the connection between the Spirit and the Word. Only then will they come with expectancy because they will know what to pray for and they will know what can happen when the Spirit ministers through the Word.

Second, teach the church that the Holy Spirit can be quenched and grieved. Sin in the body hinders reception of the Word of God. Just as preachers can have kinks in their connection with the Holy Spirit, so can a congregation. Only through repentance and confession can a heart be made ready to receive God's Word. Teach your people to come to worship with their sins confessed and cleansed by the blood of Jesus, and offer a time in the worship before the preaching of the Word for repentance and consecration.

The third truth the congregation needs to be taught is that the goal of all preaching is the glory of God. Jesus says in John 15:8, "This is to my Father's glory, that you bear much fruit, showing yourselves to be my disciples." The congregation needs to be taught that the ultimate goal of coming to church is not to hear a sermon. The ultimate goal of coming to church is to hear the Word of God preached in worship so that the indwelling Spirit in the life of every believer takes the preached Word and turns it into spiritual fruit that brings glory to God.

Fourth, teach the congregation to pray. Teach them how to pray for the preparation of their heart to receive the Word of God properly and obediently. I believe the single greatest obstacle to the movement of God's Spirit in our churches is lack of prayer. Some churches don't even pray during worship services anymore because it is considered "down time" and slows down the flow of the service. Prayer is now "in the way" of the worship service, so do it quickly, get it over with up front, squeeze it in right before the offering; but whatever you do, don't disrupt the flow of the service. We know all too well how to pray for the sick and the bereaved, so why not teach them how to pray for their own sanctification and growth?

Congregations who expect the movement of the Spirit of God must pray fervently and consistently for the Holy Spirit to glorify Christ and manifest his transformative power. Prayer is the key that opens the heart of the congregation to the spiritual dynamics at work in worship and preaching and sensitizes them to the transforming effects of the Spirit.

The Congregation and Sin: Hindering the Spirit's Work

I wonder sometimes as a pastor if we need to install a sin detector at the main entrance of the church so people can pass through it every week before they sit down and listen to the message. Could you imagine if such a device detained a woman at the door because she gossiped during the week with her neighbor, and as a result she cannot enter the service because her sin might quench the Spirit's work in the church? Imagine a businessman who stole from his corporation that week being detained at the sin detector: "Sir, we cannot let you in until you repent of your sin. Your sin could keep us all from experiencing God's best for our church." God still takes sin seriously. But does the church?

Paul tells us in 1 Corinthians 5 that it takes just a little sin to ruin the whole batch of dough. The preaching of the Word of God takes place in relationship to the dynamic of the body known as the church. Since preaching does not take place in a vacuum, the health of the body—the church—is a contributing factor. Preachers who are itinerants go to one church and preach and sense a freedom and responsiveness in the congregation. They preach to another church and sense a roadblock right away. What's the difference? Just a little bit of sin can hinder the body dynamic. Just a little bit of anger. Just a little bit of jealousy. Just a little bit of sexual promiscuity. Just a little bit of pride. Often it is the poor health of the congregation that affects their reception of God's Word.

I also wonder what we as preachers would do if we set off the sin detector: "Pastor, as long as you remain bitter toward that person on the personnel committee, God will not bless you, your family, or your church." Maybe one reason our churches take sin so lightly is that we take it so lightly as well. Do we pass through the sin detector daily and ask for cleansing and forgiveness according to 1 John 1:9? Since Spirit-led preaching hinges on the spiritual dynamics of the Holy Spirit, the congregation and the preacher must guard themselves against any impediment to the Spirit's work. We do have a resident sin detector, by the way. His name is the Holy Spirit.

The Spirit and the Invitation

It is beyond the scope of this chapter to investigate the differences of opinion regarding the public invitation. I am not seeking to defend the invitation, nor am I trying to evaluate the effectiveness of different types of the public invitation such as the altar call, the counseling room, or the response card. My experience has been that different contexts naturally call for different types of response times, but even that decision must be Spirit led.

Spirit-led preaching is not dogmatic about the type of response called for in any given sermon. What Spirit-led preaching is dogmatic about is that we boldly and unapologetically call for a response to the preached Word of God. When we call for a response, we are partnering with the Spirit's transformative purpose by calling our audience to make a Spirit-led response to the Spirit-inspired truth we are preaching.

I believe a biblical foundation for the call to commitment or public invitation is found in Acts 2:37–38, where at the end of the message people were literally coming to the apostles and asking, "Brothers, what shall we do?" I love this text because of what we don't read: "And Peter said to them, 'Every head bowed, every eye closed, nobody looking around. If you are here this morning and you've never trusted . . .'" Have you ever asked God for a sure sign that the Spirit of God was moving and ministering in a genuine way? Acts 2:37–38 gives you one sure way to tell: If your audience comes to you and asks you what they need to do before you even finish preaching your message, then *the Spirit of God is working!* The sad thing is that some of us would get offended if the Spirit moved and interrupted our message. Can you imagine Peter, led by finishing the sermon and not the Spirit, saying to these people, "Not now folks, I'm busy. Sit back down. I've got one more subpoint to cover and then a cliffhanger of a conclusion. Just about ten more minutes and I'll be through."

These people in Acts 2:37 were convinced they needed what Peter was offering them in his message, and they were convinced they needed it *now.* This is the Spirit's urgency for preaching. They heard the gospel, and they were ready to respond. We must preach with conviction, believing the Spirit is actively working in the hearts and minds of our listeners and moving them to respond appropriately to the Spirit's truth.

The Congregation and Application

Spirit-led preaching banks on the truth that the Spirit of God will continue to apply the preached Word long after the sermon is over. This is why I have strategically placed application after the invitation. Application is essential to Spirit-led preaching because it aligns powerfully with the Spirit's transformative purpose. Application is also demanded by the Spirit-intended function of Scripture revealed in 2 Timothy 3:16, where God's Word is said to be "useful" or "profitable" for equipping us for life.

John Stott, in his book *Preaching between Two Worlds,* establishes the preacher's task as bridge building between the biblical world and the contemporary world. I believe the key architect of the bridge is the Holy Spirit, who helps us see the connection to the blueprint of the biblical world and apply it within the context of the contemporary world. Application is not a *step* or *part* of sermon development; application in its purest form is preaching, and therefore preaching at its core level is the application of biblical truth to life.

I define *application* as "the Holy Spirit's ministry of constantly bringing the preached Word of God to memory and pinning it to the hearts of those we preach to so that spiritual transformation continually takes place." Some of the sweetest words a preacher will hear from his sheep are, "Do you remember a few months ago, when you said that we need to forgive . . .?" You probably don't remember your exact words, but the Spirit took the biblical truth you preached and let it simmer in the hearts of your flock until finally they made the proper application and response. That is why I believe application is not measured by one message but over a lifetime.

Spirit-led preaching also recognizes that the Holy Spirit is the one who ultimately applies the Word to the deepest parts of a listener's soul, a place we certainly cannot reach with our finite limitations as preachers. Our definition of Spirit-led preaching incorporates by design the Spirit's ministry of applying God's Word: *With a view to applying the text by means of the convicting power of the Holy Spirit first to the preacher's own heart and then to the hearts of those who hear.* The Spirit first applies the changes demanded by the text in our own lives because when we study God's Word we will be convicted. So we are partnering with the Spirit's conviction in hopes of biblical change that lasts long after the sermon is over.

In one sense the Spirit makes application while we are preaching God's Word. For example, during the application of a sermon on reconciliation from 2 Corinthians 5, we might say, "This afternoon, there's someone you need to call. There's someone you need to take the initiative with, someone you need to reconcile with." We cannot pinpoint exactly who that person may be, but the Holy Spirit can and does pinpoint exactly who that person is for each person who is listening to the indwelling Spirit within them. But the key is what they do after they leave the church building because it's then that the Spirit must continue his work of application and press the believer for obedience to what was initiated during the sermon. They still have to pick up the phone and call.

What we are doing in application is displaying how the truth of the Word of God shows up in real life. So we paint pictures of what this truth looks like in real life. We give examples. We ground the truth in specifics and stay away from the abstract. The Spirit of God contextualizes our application and specifies it for each listener, calling to remembrance some episode or some need, and then places the needed response upon the heart of the people.

Partnering with the Holy Spirit in application means we let him be the one to fill in the blanks for a person's life. We lay out for our listeners the general application, perhaps give them some examples from contemporary life, and then trust the Holy Spirit to fill in the blanks for their own specific life. Preachers who try to fill in the blanks for their listeners tend to come across as pushy, manipulative, and legalistic. Rather than trust the Spirit, they try to *be* the Spirit. Teach the audience the truth of the text—God expects purity of mind in all our thinking—and then apply it by saying, "This text applies to what we allow to come into our minds. Our television viewing habits must line up with what Paul is saying here in Philippians 4:8–9." But let the Spirit fill in the blanks and convict them about their own questionable viewing habits and whether their favorite shows line up with the moral grid of Philippians 4:8–9.

Legalistic preaching fills in the blanks for the people and does not build disciples. Spirit-led preaching trusts the Spirit to make the connection and builds mature, Spirit-filled, fruit-producing disciples. Tearful stories with guilty endings may stir people for a moment, but only the Spirit's stirring causes people to change forever. You've probably preached long enough to know that preacher-induced guilt may work for a Sunday but it fizzles fast come Monday.

Keys to Spirit-Led Application

The first key to partnering with the Spirit in application is that the biblical truth we are preaching must first be applied to our own hearts. We must preach from hearts that have already been touched and transformed by the truth. We've already begun the application process in our own lives so that we are calling *for* transformation out of a heart that is *in* transformation as we preach. It's not wrong for a preacher to say, "After studying this text this week, the Lord put it on my heart to change a few things in our house about the way we do our prayer and family devotions." I think people need to hear from a preacher who is authentically living out the truth in their personal and family life.

My experience has been that the church's evaluation of your sincerity and your authenticity does not happen primarily on Sunday morning during the sermon. It happens throughout the week as they observe you and your family and see you interact with people outside the church. They want to see real-life application in everyday life—not in the pulpit where it's safe. If we desire to preach "heart to heart," then we must first apply the truth to our own hearts so that our people will see the power of the Word to transform us.

The second key to partnering with the Holy Spirit in application is to understand that the Spirit's knowledge knows no limits. He is God! So I need the Spirit's help in application because as a preacher I am limited. I am limited in time so I cannot make every possible life application from the text I am preaching. I am limited by authorial intent, which means I cannot falsely apply a text in such a way that I would contradict the biblical writer. I am not free to make any application I want to make. I need to demonstrate its legitimacy from the text. I am also limited in my knowledge of my audience. I don't know everything that happened to them during the week, and I don't know the deepest needs of every heart that looks my way on Sunday morning. We can and should know some of those needs from spending time with the sheep, but we cannot know all. So the fact is we need help.

The Spirit, not the preacher, is free to apply the Word as he sees fit because the Spirit, not the preacher, is God. You've probably had that experience where the Spirit of God surprised you by the way he used your message. You are talking to someone after the service, and they share how God spoke to them through the message, and you are reflecting over the message in your mind and saying to yourself, *I must be losing my mind. I don't recall saying that in my message.* Just rejoice that the Spirit of God took your message and spoke into someone's life in a way that you could never do.

The third key to partnering with the Holy Spirit in application is the fact that we come into alignment with the Spirit's ultimate purpose, that we bear fruit to God's glory. In other words, as we bring our messages into alignment with the profitability of all Scripture (2 Tim. 3:16), our messages conform to the Spirit's transforming purpose. The Spirit takes the Word of God and uses it in the life of a believer in order to produce fruit: love, joy, peace, patience, kindness, goodness, faithfulness, gentleness, and self-control. So one of the key questions for us as preachers is this: "In what way does the text I am preaching from serve the Spirit's purpose to bear much fruit in my listeners?"

In other words, what kind of fruit is called for in my sermon text? Preach from Psalm 150, and you are coming into alignment with the Spirit's desire for us to have the fruit of joy in worship. Preach from Psalm 73, and you are calling your people to faithfulness, even while the ungodly around us prosper. Identify the Galatians 5:22 fruit your preaching text is filled with, and pray that your message will bear the Spirit's desired fruit in the lives of your listeners.

Conclusion

The message is delivered, the invitation has come and gone, and the congregation is on its way home. Has the Holy Spirit finished his work? Though we often talk of the Spirit moving and working in a worship service, in a real sense the work of the Spirit never stops. The Holy Spirit constantly and continuously takes the truth of God's Word and produces Spirit-filled living in the believer's life. I find it refreshing as a preacher of God's Word to know that the work of the Spirit will take the message far beyond Sunday morning. Our preaching is not in vain because the Spirit takes the Word we preach and uses it to produce disciples.

Since we partner with the Holy Spirit, we don't need to follow all our church members to their places of work or into their homes, saying, "Remember what I said Sunday. Remember what I said three weeks ago about that." It's the indwelling Holy Spirit who brings to remembrance God's truth for believers to apply to their specific life situations. Praise God for such a gift to our preaching!

Chapter 9

The Holy Spirit and the Anointing: Understanding the Spirit's Empowerment for Preaching

The gospel is preached in the ears of all; it only comes with power to some. The power that is in the gospel does not lie in the eloquence of the preacher; otherwise men would be the converters of souls. Nor does it lie in the preacher's learning; otherwise it would consist in the wisdom of men. We might preach till our tongues rotted, till we should exhaust our lungs and die, but never a soul would be converted unless there were a mysterious power going with it—the Holy Ghost changing the will of man. Oh Sirs! We might as well preach to stone walls as preach to humanity unless the Holy Ghost be with the Word, to give it power to convert the soul.

—*Charles Haddon Spurgeon*

Some of you cheated. I knew you would. You skipped the first eight chapters and turned here first to see what I had to say about the anointing. I can hear you saying, "Cut to the chase. Get to the anointing. What is it, and how do I get it?" Although I don't believe the anointing can be reduced to a formula, I do believe there are certain characteristics that tend to surround the Spirit's anointing for preaching. But if you came to this chapter

126

seeking "the seven easy steps to Spirit-anointed preaching," you will be greatly disappointed. You cannot take a shortcut approach to God the Holy Spirit. There's no easy or secret way to incorporate the Spirit's ministry into our preaching, and steps and formulas would only mechanize what according to Scripture is clearly a spiritual dynamic (1 Cor. 2:4).

I want to offer three disclaimers before we begin this chapter.

First, this chapter is heavy with quotations, primarily because I want you to be able to read the firsthand accounts of preachers who have described the anointing in their own words. Hearing preachers describe their own experiences proved to be a great challenge and encouragement to my own preaching, and I pray it will prove to be the same for yours.

Second, space did not allow me to take a concordance approach to the anointing, so I do not trace the anointing throughout the Bible. For example, items in the temple are spoken of as "anointed." Craftsmen who worked on the temple were "anointed." The sick are "anointed" in James 5. So by intention, I have only focused this chapter on the Scriptures most closely related to preaching.

Third, I do not interact with the popular charismatic understanding of the anointing as mysteriously breathing on people or touching people and then becoming "slain in the Spirit." Though popularized on television and personalized for every believer, the fact that this kind of so-called anointing makes so much of the individual and not God and, though said to be "miraculous" can be "learned and taught in five easy steps," makes me discount this understanding of the anointing altogether.

Confusion Surrounding the Anointing

The most confusing and controversial subject related to the Holy Spirit and preaching is the spiritual dynamic popularly known as "the anointing." Most of the confusion stems from the subjective nature of the anointing as well as the imprecise terminology used to describe the phenomenon. Add to that mixture the misinterpretation and misapplication of biblical passages, and we've got ourselves a theological Pandora's box that allows almost anything to pass for the Spirit's work in the church today. Furthermore, when preachers are asked what the anointing is, they typically find their experiences difficult to objectify or articulate. Spurgeon himself struggled to put the Spirit's power for preaching into words:

> What is it? I wonder how long we might beat our brains before we could plainly put into words what is meant by *preaching with unction;* yet he who preaches knows its presence, and he who hears soon detects its absence; such is the mystery of the anointing; we know, but we cannot tell others what it is.[1]

I will approach the anointing in the following manner. First, the chapter will point out the varying differences in understanding regarding the anointing. Second, I will make a case for using the term *empowerment* as an alternative to the *anointing*. Third, I will define the Spirit's empowerment for preaching from both biblical and experiential sources. Fourth, the chapter will point out the helps and hindrances that influence the Spirit's empowerment, and finally I will conclude by examining the frequency of the Spirit's empowerment.

Anointing: Fact or Fiction?

The unfamiliarity many preachers have regarding the Spirit's power for preaching is lamentable. One cause is ignorance. As preachers we are called to be theologians, but as we pointed out earlier, the doctrine of the Holy Spirit is overlooked and underdeveloped in many theologies of preaching. Jay Adams challenges us to do something about our theological ineptitude regarding the Holy Spirit:

> There has been a conspiracy of ignorance in which words and phrases have been uttered again and again as though the speakers and the listeners knew perfectly well what they were talking about, when all the while they did not. As a homiletician who has been at fault in

---

1. Charles Haddon Spurgeon, *Lectures to My Students* (Carlisle, Pa.: Banner of Truth, 1979), 50.

this matter, I believe something must be done. It is time the whole matter was cleared up."[2]

My own research confirms Adams's observation: preachers often talk about the Spirit with vague generalities and tip their theological hats to acknowledge their need of the Spirit, but when it comes to specifics and theological depth, you find few satisfying explanations or answers. Homiletics textbooks lack consensus and clarity as well. They are filled with various and loosely defined terms used to describe the anointing such as "unction," "empowerment," "possession," "filling," "vitality," and "baptism in the Spirit." Disparity, disagreement, and even outright denial form the spectrum of opinions regarding this controversial topic.

Based on my research on the Spirit's anointing for preaching, I believe in most instances we are describing the same phenomenon but using different terms. Nuances exist—both theological and experiential—but more often than not, the reference is to the Spirit's supernatural power attending the proclamation of the Word of God. Some tend to define the anointing in terms of its results. Others define it in terms of the effect upon the preacher's delivery. Still others define the anointing in terms of its impact on the congregation.

Some, such as Alex Montoya, deny the anointing exists in its popularly understood form. This school of thought relies more on the gifting and equipping of the Spirit, rather than on the Spirit's supernatural and mysterious empowerment. In his book *Preaching with Passion,* Montoya writes:

> It is my conclusion that such a thing [the anointing] does not exist. We should be relieved of this unspeakable burden placed upon us by those who teach this about preaching. Every example given of men who preached with unction were men endowed with manifold speaking and intellectual abilities.[3]

Although I disagree with Montoya's explanation that the anointing can be accounted for through God-given "manifold speaking and

---

2. Jay Adams, *Preaching to the Heart* (Grand Rapids: Zondervan, 1983), 13.
3. Alex Montoya, *Preaching with Passion* (Grand Rapids: Kregel, 2000), 35.

intellectual abilities," I do concur that we need to clarify what it rightly means to be empowered by the Spirit for preaching. For many preachers the ambiguity surrounding the anointing can be frustrating and misleading. You don't read Lloyd-Jones on the anointing for too long before you start asking yourself, "Could this ever happen to me? This is incredible!"

Montoya's statement that men who preached with unction in the past were "endowed with manifold speaking and intellectual abilities" is too simplistic. What about Paul in Corinth? He shunned the approach of the rhetoricians of his day, who relied upon their "speaking and intellectual abilities." To reduce powerful preaching to talent—even God-given talent—seems to me to overlook the Spirit's ministries made available to us in preaching. D. L. Moody was not known for his eloquence or his intellectual acumen, but he was known for powerful preaching!

The anointing for preaching is hard to define and maintains a sense of mystery about it, but that admission is no reason to conclude that it does not exist. We cannot deny that Old Testament prophets such as Elijah and Jeremiah spoke with God's anointing (1 Kings 17:2; Jer. 50:1). In the New Testament, John the Baptist, Jesus, Peter, Paul, and John all preached with God's anointing (Luke 1:15; 4:18; Acts 4:8; 13:9; Rev. 1:10). So to deny the anointing and instead point to the giftedness of men as the explanation for the Spirit's empowerment does not square with Scripture or with history.

In stark contrast to Montoya, Martyn Lloyd-Jones affirms the anointing as a special "unction" given to preachers. Referencing Jesus' command to the disciples to stay in Jerusalem until they received "power from on high" (Luke 24:49), Lloyd-Jones states:

> You would have thought these men therefore were now in a perfect position to go out and preach; but according to our Lord's teaching, they were not. They seem to have all the necessary knowledge, but that knowledge is not sufficient. Something further is needed, is indeed essential. The knowledge indeed is vital for you cannot be witnesses without it, but to be more effective witnesses you need the power and the

unction and the demonstration of the Spirit in addition. Now if this was necessary for these men, how much more is necessary for all others who try to preach these things?[4]

Jones's line of reasoning is convincing. Jesus clearly indicated to the disciples that they needed power from on high—supernatural power—to preach the gospel to all the nations. The power that Jesus told the disciples to wait for at the end of Luke's Gospel was then manifested throughout the book of Acts. Acts 4:8 states that "Peter, filled with the Holy Spirit, said . . ." and Acts 13:9 says, "Paul, filled with the Holy Spirit . . . said. . . ." What Luke was trying to establish is the critical link between the Spirit and proclamation because wherever we see proclamation taking place in Luke-Acts, we find the Spirit.

Does the preaching of the gospel today still require the attendant power of the Holy Spirit? Can we expect the "proclamation and Spirit" paradigm established in Luke-Acts to accompany our preaching of the gospel today? I believe that the Spirit and proclamation are still necessary because we are preaching the same message and we are up against the same sin-hardened hearts that can only be opened by the Holy Spirit (Acts 16:14). The Spirit's illumination, testimonium, conviction, guidance, and Christological witness are all available and necessary for the preaching of the gospel today. I do not believe that the Spirit's power for preaching ended in the apostolic age. Just as Jesus was empowered by the Spirit to reveal to us the glory of the Father, so the Spirit empowers us to bring glory to the Son. By the Spirit, Jesus completed the work the Father had given him to do on earth (John 17:4), and by the same Spirit we work to complete the mission Jesus has given to us to do until every knee shall bow and every tongue confess that Jesus is Lord.

I want you to notice something interesting: The Bible says in 1 Corinthians 12:3 that no one can say, "Jesus is Lord" except by the Holy Spirit. The Bible also says in Romans 10:14 that they cannot call on the one in whom they have not heard, and they cannot hear

---

4. Martyn Lloyd-Jones, *Preaching and Preachers* (Grand Rapids: Zondervan, 1971), 308.

unless someone preaches to them. This vital connection between preacher, Spirit, and "Jesus is Lord" demonstrates biblically that we must have the Spirit's empowerment for preaching, and we must have preachers who unashamedly preach the gospel of Jesus Christ.

The Anointing as Spirit-Filled Living

The Spirit's anointing for preaching is grounded in the Spirit-filled life. Although the Spirit's anointing receives a separate chapter in this book, I cannot overemphasize the fact that the Spirit's empowerment for preaching grows out of Spirit-filled living. If the preacher's life is not characterized by love, joy, peace, patience, kindness, goodness, gentleness, faithfulness, and self-control, then his preaching will not be characterized by the Spirit's power. The Spirit must first mark the preacher's life before he marks his preaching. The fruit of the Holy Spirit in our lives gives birth to the power of the Holy Spirit in our preaching.

In Colossians 1:9, Paul's prayer for the church begins by asking that the believers in Colossae be filled "with the knowledge of his will." The verb speaks of a continuous filling and carries the idea that whatever we are filled with will ultimately be what controls us. Paul is saying to let the knowledge of God's will—his Word—fill and control us. The Spirit's anointing works in much the same way. When our lives are Spirit filled, we are Spirit led. The Spirit fills us and controls us, and God takes us in our surrendered state and blesses us with the attendant power of the Holy Spirit for preaching.

Ephesians 5:18 talks about the ability of alcohol to come into our bodies and control us: "Do not get drunk on wine, which leads to debauchery. Instead, be filled with the Spirit." In both Colossians 1:9 and Ephesians 5:18, the idea is one of possession and control. Colossians 1:9 calls us to be filled and controlled by the knowledge of his will as it is revealed in Scripture—the Word. Ephesians 5:18 calls us to be filled with and controlled by the indwelling Holy Spirit—the Spirit. So the preacher who is anointed for preaching and empowered by the Holy Spirit will be filled and controlled by both Word and Spirit.

Vines and Shaddix agree:

The anointing is the spiritual fervor that flows through a man in the preaching event. Though the effects of this divine work often are not noticed until the delivery of the sermon, the man of God must build his entire preaching ministry on its presence. Consequently, attention must be given to the need for this anointing long before the sermon-building process begins.[5]

If our hearts are deeply convinced that apart from the Spirit's empowerment our preaching and our message are powerless, then we will be burdened *as a way of life* with absolute dependence upon the Spirit of God for all things.

Defining the Anointing: The Case for Empowerment

The problem of defining the anointing begins when we observe that the anointing spoken of in 1 John 2:27 and 2 Corinthians 1:21 applies to all believers, not just preachers. Believers who are indwelled by the Holy Spirit are all anointed in the biblical sense and have all been given *charismata,* or spiritual gifts. This raises the question, are preachers anointed in a different sense for preaching? Is there an anointing for believers but then a different anointing for preachers? Commenting on 1 John 2:20, Akin states: "John affirms that the anointing (Spirit), received by believing that Jesus is the Christ, the Son of God, teaches them the truth of the gospel. . . . what the Spirit teaches . . . is true and can be trusted without reservation."[6]

I do not think this passage is teaching us about a special super-anointing for preachers. I do believe that the 1 John 2:20 anointing we have as believers—the Spirit's internal witness to the truthfulness of the gospel—should carry over into our preaching and produce confidence and conviction within us. But to build an entire concept of the anointing for preaching on this verse alone seems forced at best. How then can preachers justify using the word *anointing* in reference to preaching?

---

5. Vines and Shaddix, *Power in the Pulpit,* 64.

6. Daniel L. Akin, *1, 2, 3 John,* New American Commentary (Nashville: Broadman & Holman, 2001), 126.

In Acts 10:38, the Bible says concerning Jesus, "God anointed Jesus of Nazareth with the Holy Spirit and power, and how he went around doing good and healing all who were under the power of the devil, because God was with him." The Greek word for "anointed" in this passage is *chrisen* and carries with it the idea of being divinely commissioned. At his baptism Christ received such a commission as the Spirit descended upon him, signaling the beginning of his ministry. What Luke is affirming in Acts 10:38 is that Jesus was commissioned in two clear ways: with the Holy Spirit and with power. Although all believers are anointed according to 1 John 2:20 and 2 Corinthians 1:21 and have the Spirit's internal, indwelling testimony, other passages such as Luke 4:18; Acts 10:38; and 1 Corinthians 2:4 broaden the concept of the anointing to include the idea of the Spirit's empowerment for proclamation.

I want to suggest that we move away from using *anointing* to describe the Spirit's work in preaching and instead talk of the Spirit's *empowerment*. Empowerment seems to be broad enough to capture the dynamic of the Spirit's power for preaching and avoids the confusion and apprehension created by the stereotyped term *anointing*. Furthermore, terms such as *anointing* and *Spirit filled* are unsatisfying because all believers are Spirit filled and anointed in the biblical sense.

As we turn to the biblical evidence next, I think you will conclude that one single phrase or word does not do justice to the dynamic of the Spirit in preaching. Perhaps that's where we need to land on this issue: The Spirit is beyond boxing in and in some sense is beyond our definitions. His ministry for preaching cannot be captured in one word, as we will see.

Biblical Support for the Spirit's Empowerment

Jesus. First, the ministry of Jesus is distinctively characterized by the Spirit's involvement and empowerment. Matthew 3:16 states, "As soon as Jesus was baptized, he went up out of the water. At that moment heaven was opened, and he saw the Spirit of God descending like a dove and lighting on him." Soon after his baptism, Luke 4:1–2 states that the Holy Spirit directed and emboldened Jesus for the temptations he would face: "Jesus, full of the Holy Spirit, returned from the Jordan and was led by the Spirit in the desert, where for forty days he was tempted by the devil." After returning from the desert, Jesus launched his preaching ministry by proclaiming God's Spirit was upon him to preach: "The scroll of the prophet Isaiah was handed to him. Unrolling it, he found the place where it is written: 'The Spirit of the Lord is on me, because he has anointed me to preach good news to the poor'" (Luke 4:17–18).

Notice that Jesus was reading from the scroll containing Isaiah's prophecy (Word) while at the same time announcing the Spirit's empowerment (Spirit) on his life. Jesus is the ultimate fulfillment of Word and Spirit, as evidenced in John 3:34: "For the one whom God has sent speaks the words of God, for God gives the Spirit without limit." Finally, prior to the beginning of the disciples' preaching of the gospel recorded in the book of Acts, Jesus stated in Luke 24:49 that he was sending the Spirit to accompany the preaching of the Word: "I am going to send you what my Father has promised; but stay in the city until you have been clothed with power from on high."

1 John 2:27. John states,

> As for you, the anointing you received from him remains in you, and you do not need anyone to teach you. But as his anointing teaches you about all things and as that anointing is real, not counterfeit—just as it has taught you, remain in him (1 John 2:27).

Although all believers have the anointing spoken of in this text, its implications do carry over into preaching. MacArthur observed that anointing in its historical context refers to the rubbing in of an ointment, and therefore the picture in this text is "the Spirit as the One who resides within the believer and permeates his life with God's truth."[7]

I believe the anointing referred to in 1 John 2:27 is referring to the Spirit's John 16:14 ministry of guiding every believer into truth. In this sense those who preach the gospel are said to be "anointed" because they are permeated by the truth they are studying and preaching. We need the Spirit to rub in his inspired truth deep into our souls to bring depth and richness to our preaching. Powerful

---

7. John MacArthur, *Whatever Happened to the Holy Spirit* (Chicago: Moody, 1989), 17.

preaching is "anointed preaching" in this sense: what the Spirit rubs into our hearts comes running out of mouths, for out of the overflow of the heart, the mouth speaks.

Ephesians 6:19. A second key biblical text for understanding the Spirit's empowerment is Ephesians 6:19. Paul stated, "Pray also for me, that whenever I open my mouth, words may be given me so that I will fearlessly make known the mystery of the gospel." Paul clearly had in mind here boldness for proclamation of the gospel, although the Holy Spirit is not directly referenced in the verse. However, the overall context of Ephesians 6 is spiritual warfare, which definitely involves the Spirit. Paul instructed the Ephesians to use the Word of God as their sword, but he also reminded them of their need for supernatural power indicated by his prayer.

One characteristic of Spirit-empowered preaching is "fearlessness" or "boldness," not because we are personally bold and courageous but because the Spirit who indwells us is bold and courageous (2 Tim. 1:7). Adams queries, "What is boldness? The Greek word, *parresia,* means freedom in speaking, openness, willingness to be frank; it is plain speech that is unencumbered by fear."[8] The boldness of our proclamation stems from the Spirit-given confidence that the Word of God is a powerful sword that can penetrate the deepest darkness of sin.

Acts. The book of Acts broadens the Spirit's empowerment for preaching by referring over and over again to the Spirit's filling for proclamation. Acts 4:8 states, "Then Peter, *filled* with the Holy Spirit, *said*" (emphasis added). Acts 13:9 reads, "Then Saul, who was also called Paul, *filled* with the Holy Spirit, looked straight at Elymas and *said*" (emphasis added). Acts 4:31 declares, "After they prayed, the place where they were meeting was shaken. And they were all *filled* with the Holy Spirit and *spoke* the word of God boldly" (emphasis added). The anointing in Acts is represented as "filling power." What caused them to speak with boldness? What caused them to preach with power? Luke wants us to see the pattern that these early gospel preachers were clearly filled and controlled by the Holy Spirit.

---

8. Adams, *Preaching to the Heart,* 16.

For us as preachers today, to be empowered by the Holy Spirit means that we are filled and controlled by the power of the Holy Spirit. Spirit-empowered preaching comes out of a heart and mind that are dominated by the Spirit. When we are filled with the Spirit, the Spirit controls us inwardly, and we submit all of our desires, attitudes, and motivations to him because we are walking according to the Spirit. His agenda for glorifying Christ becomes our agenda in preaching. We die to the flesh in order that we can live according to the Spirit. I believe this type of submission to the Spirit's control is the foundation for Spirit-led preaching.

Spirit Baptism. Before leaving the discussion of the biblical data, one last consideration should be given to R. A. Torrey's understanding of the anointing as Spirit baptism. He cites John the Baptist's testimony concerning Jesus: "I baptize you with water, but he will baptize you with the Holy Spirit" (Mark 1:8). Torrey believed that the baptism of the Spirit happens after regeneration. He writes, "It is evident that the baptism with the Holy Spirit is an operation of the Spirit distinct from and additional to His regenerating work."[9] Torrey makes this distinction between the Spirit's regenerating work and the Spirit's baptizing work, by stating that the regeneration is for salvation, and Spirit baptism is being "fitted for service."[10]

Torrey's understanding of the need for us to be fitted for service by the Holy Spirit's power is right; we do need an impartation of power. My reservation is where Torrey places the reception of that power—in Spirit baptism some time after conversion. In Romans 6, Paul established once and for all that we are baptized into Christ at the moment of regeneration by the Holy Spirit. Scripture nowhere indicates a secondary work of the Holy Spirit as necessary for the impartation of divine power. Ephesians 5:18 does say that believers are to be continually filled with the Spirit—a present-tense, continuous experience of the filling that took place at regeneration, not a separate, unique experience.

---

9. R. A. Torrey, *The Person and Work of the Holy Spirit* (1910; repr., Grand Rapids: Zondervan, 1974), 149.

10. Ibid., 150.

Characteristics of the Spirit's Empowerment

Before I begin this section, I want to remind you that these descriptions you are about to read are firsthand accounts of the Spirit's empowerment. Some you will agree with; others you may not. Some you will identify with based on your own preaching experience, and others you will struggle to relate to. We are seeking to answer this question: what does the Spirit's empowerment look like when experienced in the act of preaching?

1. *Freedom.* The first characteristic of Spirit-empowered preaching is the freedom the preacher experiences during the act of preaching. Sargent described the experience:

> It is the afflatus of the Spirit resting on the speaker. It is "power from on high." It is the preacher gliding on eagles wings, soaring high, swooping low, carrying and being carried along by a dynamic other than his own. His consciousness of what is happening is not obliterated. He is not in a trance. He is being worked on but is aware that he is still working. He is being spoken through but he knows he is still speaking. The words are his but the facility with which they come compels him to realize that the source is beyond himself.[11]

The heightened sense of awareness given by the Spirit intensifies the flow and precision of the message as well. Azurdia explains this intensity:

> There have been those occasional moments in preaching when I have become mindful of an other-worldly kind of enablement; when my thoughts concerning the Scriptures were suddenly made free from all apparent impediments, when my affections for Jesus Christ and the well-being of souls were unusually intensified, when words and phrases came with ease and precision.[12]

---

11. Tony Sargent, *The Sacred Anointing* (Wheaton, Ill.: Crossway, 1994), 29.

12. Arturo Azurdia, *Spirit-Empowered Preaching* (Ross-shire, Great Britain: Mentor, 1998), 179.

The Spirit's empowerment gives intensity and clarity, resulting in a preacher who passionately delivers the Word with urgency and conviction. Kent Hughes states the freedom the Spirit gives the preacher this way:

> There are times when I am preaching that I have especially sensed the pleasure of God. I usually become aware of it through the unnatural silence. The ever-present coughing ceases and the pews stop creaking, bringing an almost physical quiet to the sanctuary—through which my words sail like arrows. I experience a heightened eloquence, so that the cadence and volume of my voice intensify the truth I am preaching. There is nothing quite like it—the Holy Spirit filling one's sails.[13]

I do believe that the Holy Spirit gives us a freedom in the pulpit. I think in my own preaching I sense the freedom of the Spirit when I surrender my fear of disappointing or displeasing people and instead focus totally on obeying God and pleasing him in my message. I stop thinking about myself and overanalyzing myself, and I just focus on preaching the Word and bringing glory to Christ, which the Spirit is glad to bless.

2. *Vitality.* A second characteristic of Spirit-empowered preaching is vitality. Vitality refers to preaching that is alive and full of vibrant life and is the essence of Hebrews 4:12, which states that the Word is living and active and sharp. The Word of God shows itself to be the living Word through the mouthpiece of the preacher and the testimony of the Spirit. The power of the proclaimed Word brings life, sustains life, and empowers life. The preacher comes alive because he is caught up in the power of preaching the Word. The Word is alive, as its meaning is exposited and its transforming power becomes manifest. The Spirit is alive, as he infuses preacher and listener with his divine enablement—the preacher to proclaim powerfully and the listener to hear properly.

3. *Power.* A third characteristic of the Spirit's empowerment is the idea of unction or power. From this perspective the Spirit's

---

13. R. Kent Hughes and Bryan Chappell, *1 and 2 Timothy and Titus,* Preaching the Word Series (Wheaton: Crossway Books), 13.

anointing supersedes natural human ability and talent. It is grounded in Paul's thought found in 1 Corinthians 2:4–5: "My message and my preaching were not with wise and persuasive words, but with a demonstration of the Spirit's power, so that your faith might not rest on men's wisdom, but on God's power." Martyn Lloyd-Jones comments:

> What is meant by this "unction" or "anointing" of the Holy Spirit? . . . It is the Spirit falling upon the preacher in a special manner. It is an access of power. It is God giving power, and enabling, through the Spirit, to the preacher in order that he may do this work in a manner that lifts it up beyond the efforts and endeavors of man to a position in which the preacher is being used by the Spirit and becomes a channel through whom the Spirit works.[14]

4. *Possession.* A fourth characteristic of the Spirit's empowerment is possession. Possession takes place in the sense that an outside power greater than the preacher's own ability takes control of the preacher. Typically, the idea of possession is limited to the actual delivery of the message. Lloyd-Jones again comments:

> How does one know the unction of the Spirit? It gives clarity of thought, clarity of speech, ease of utterance, a great sense of authority and confidence as you are preaching, an awareness of a power not your own thrilling through the whole of your being, and an indescribable sense of joy. You are a man "possessed," you are taken hold of, and taken up. I like to put it like this—and I know of nothing on earth that is comparable to this feeling— that when this happens you have a feeling that you are not actually doing the preaching, you are looking on at yourself in amazement as this is happening. It is not your effort; you are just the instrument, the channel, the vehicle: the Spirit is using you, and you are looking on in great enjoyment and astonishment.[15]

---

14. Martyn Lloyd-Jones, *Preaching and Preachers*, 305.
15. Ibid., 324.

This is why I said earlier in the book that some people wish that Lloyd-Jones had taken this type of description with him to the grave instead of publishing it for all to see! For one, the Spirit indwells us as believers, but it is clear from this description that Lloyd-Jones is talking about something more, something that comes from the outside, and something he would call "power from on high." The other controversial reference is to this idea of being taken over by the Spirit, to the degree that we are no longer the ones doing the preaching. It's as if we stop preaching and the Spirit starts.

Just in case you are ready to write off Lloyd-Jones as an anomaly, let's look at a testimony from Chuck Swindoll. He shared his similar experience of being "caught up with the Spirit" in a 1996 interview with Michael Diduit:

> Then there is the actual delivery. You've preached enough, Mike, to know there are times—I don't want this to sound spooky—but there are times I feel almost outside myself. You have that experience where you say (and even at the time you're delivering it you are thinking), "I could not have arranged these thoughts this well." I use notes when I preach and so I will look down on occasion and I'll be three pages ahead of my notes—caught up in the movement of the message. And I think the Spirit of God is doing that.[16]

Jerry Vines and Jim Shaddix also support the idea of possession and take the idea a step further by applying its effects to the congregation as well:

> Spirit-anointed preaching does something to both the preacher and people. The anointing keeps the preacher aware of a power not his own. In the best sense of the word, he is "possessed"—caught up in the message by the power of the Spirit. He becomes a channel used by the Holy Spirit. At the same time the people are gripped, moved, and convicted. When the Holy Spirit takes over in the preaching event, something miraculous happens.[17]

---

16. Chuck Swindoll, "Preaching and the Holy Spirit," in *Communicating with Power,* ed. Michael Diduit (Grand Rapids: Baker, 1996), 194–95.

17. Vines and Shaddix, *Power in the Pulpit,* 45.

Personal Testimonies and the Spirit's Empowerment

Firsthand accounts of the Spirit's empowerment in preaching are difficult to find because rarely does the subject make it into print. Sensational accounts of the Spirit's anointing sometimes intimidate preachers since that's not their experience week in and week out. Azurdia candidly shares his preaching experience:

> More commonly, however, my experience in preaching has not been so dramatic. To be sure, never once have I felt anything less than a thorough-going confidence in the integrity and authority of the biblical text. Nor have I ever felt that the act of preaching itself was perfunctory. But to suggest that I am thoroughly conscious of the effects of my preaching at the conclusion of each Lord's day would be less than honest. Though I preach to a wonderfully responsive congregation, frequently I have no immediate and personal sense of the effectiveness of my preaching.[18]

Week in and week out, most preachers can identify with Azurdia's statement. We've prayed and prepared, and we've depended on the Holy Spirit, and we put our confidence in the Word, but sometimes not much happens (at least by what we see and sense), and we question our effectiveness. One reason for this is what I call a "holy dissatisfaction" with our preaching. We replay the message in our minds, identifying all the things we left out that we should not have, all the things we added that we should have left out, and all the things that did not go right. For better or for worse, that is our tendency as preachers.

I tell my students that the desire to grow and learn from our mistakes is one that I believe God honors. But to obsess over them and fixate on them is unhealthy, counterproductive, and makes preaching to be more about our performance than the glory of God. Week in and week out, many preachers faithfully proclaim God's Word and see God do great things, but they do not experience the dramatic element of the Spirit's empowerment that others have pointed to in their preaching. My conclusion to the matter is this: I believe the Spirit's empowerment can be manifest in both faithful

---

18. Azurdia, *Spirit-Empowered Preaching*, 179.

and consistent dependency week in and week out as well as in unusual and dramatic irregularity.

Opposite Azurdia's experience, there are those whose unique and dramatic experience of the Spirit impacts them for a lifetime. Jerry Vines shares an experience that occurred while preparing a message for the 1976 Alabama Baptist State Convention. Vines recalls:

> Within a month of the time I was to deliver this message, I became aware that God was working in my heart and life in a peculiar way. The theme consumed me. I could hardly stay away from my study. Many nights I stayed up into the wee hours studying and preparing this message. Many, many times God's presence was so overwhelming as I prepared that I would actually weep. The day came for me to deliver the message. The conference to that point had been average and nothing unusual had happened. I approached my assignment with great fear and trepidation—I almost had a sense of dread. When I began to preach, however, something happened. When I was barely five minutes into the message, the Spirit of God seemed to take complete possession of me. The congregation of mostly preachers was caught up as well. I felt as if I were actually in another world looking on the event. The conference of preachers seemed to be swept along in a flood tide of joy and spiritual excitement. When I finished, we were all aware that God had visited us. Never before nor since have I been so stirred and moved by the Holy Spirit.[19]

A few years ago I had the privilege of hearing Dr. Vines in person recount this experience, and though some twenty-five years had passed since it first happened, he still could not talk about that special time without tears flowing from his eyes, and it was so powerful to see that he was still moved by the experience.

York brings a third testimony to our discussion by sharing his own experience:

---

19. Vines and Shaddix, *Power in the Pulpit,* 67.

I recall times when I have been preaching when God simply moved in and took over. I fail to comprehend it myself, let alone explain it to anyone else. The closest analogy I can use is that it is like standing outside of myself, watching myself preach, knowing that God is speaking through me in an incredible way. I used to think that those moments came almost randomly, that God seemed almost capricious. But after years of preaching and observation of myself and others, I realize that those times occur when I am most saturated with the Scripture I am preaching, convinced of its meaning, emboldened by its power, and secure in its application. I feel no strain, no duplicity, no regrets that I have not spent enough time with the Lord and the text he has given.[20]

York rightly corrects the false understanding of the Spirit's empowerment as some type of mystical randomness that "capriciously" shows up from time to time. Preaching with no regrets means we pray, we plan, we prepare, and we come expecting God to do something powerful by his Spirit with what he has given us in his Word.

Receiving the Spirit's Empowerment

What internal and external characteristics factor into the Spirit's empowerment in preaching? Is there any pattern, any particular atmosphere, in which the Spirit of God seems to attend to the preaching of the Word with more frequency? I acknowledge up front that the Spirit shows up and uses us when we least expect it. Maybe you were sick, maybe you had two weddings and three funerals and did not prepare as well, or maybe you had a crisis to deal with in your church family and were not as focused. You cannot explain it, but for some reason the Spirit of God showed up and moved greatly through you and your people. Yes, the Spirit can overcome such unusual weeks and situations, but these must be the exception, not the general rule.

---

20. Hershael York and Bert Decker, *Preaching with Bold Assurance* (Nashville: Broadman & Holman, 2003), 3.

Although there is no magic formula or secret recipe that guarantees the preacher automatically receives the empowerment of the Holy Spirit, I do believe that the faithful implementation of the Spirit-led approach to preaching that I have laid out for you in this book will at least *place* your heart in a position that the Spirit of God can use. The goal of Spirit-led preaching is to create an environment or an atmosphere in which the Spirit's empowerment is anticipated, welcomed, received, and demonstrated through the proclamation of God's Word. In a survey of the literature, the Spirit's empowerment seems to be directly associated with the following factors: prayer, fullness, faith, humility, and weakness.

Helps to the Spirit's Empowerment

Prayer. Prayer is one indicator of our absolute dependence on God. Prayer puts us in glad submission to and in communion with our source of inspiration, help, and empowerment—the Lord God. Piper acknowledged the relationship between prayer and dependence when he wrote, "The goal of preaching is utterly dependent upon the mercy of God for its fulfillment. Therefore, the preacher must labor to put his preaching under divine influence by prayer."[21] We cannot wait until we are in a jam to pray as preachers. We cannot see prayer as an add-on accessory to preaching that we do if we happen to have time. Preaching by definition means we listen to God before we speak to men.

Let the words of E. M. Bounds call you into a fresh commitment to prayer:

> The Bible preacher prays. He is filled with the Holy Spirit, filled with God's Word, and filled with faith. He has faith in God; he has faith in God's only begotten Son, his personal Savior; and he has implicit faith in God's Word. He cannot do otherwise than pray. He cannot be other than a person of prayer. The breath of his life and the throb of his heart are prayer. The Bible preacher lives by prayer, loves by prayer, and preaches

---

21. John Piper, *The Supremacy of God in Preaching* (Grand Rapids: Baker, 1990), 98.

by prayer. His bended knees in the place of secret prayer advertise what kind of preacher he is."[22]

Fullness. The book of Acts provides two different pictures of two very different men. In Acts 11:24, Barnabas is described as being "a good man, full of the Holy Spirit and faith, and a great number of people were brought to the Lord." On the other hand, Simon the magician is described in Acts 8:23 as "full of bitterness and captive to sin." Whatever we are full of will ultimately control us. This is what preaching from the overflow is all about. The overflow of the Word that has soaked into us and saturated us combines with the overflow of the Spirit's filling and leading, and the result is a preacher who out of the overflow of his heart preaches a dynamic and powerful message that is Word and Spirit filled.

Weakness and Humility. I have intentionally combined these two characteristics because they feed off each other. Weakness keeps us humble by reminding us that we are human and we are frail—but dust. Humility embraces weakness as a blessing, not as a burden, and causes us to call on the Lord for help. Weakness keeps us dependent, and dependence keeps us humble. The preacher who revels in his weakness will know the truth Paul speaks of in 2 Corinthians 12:10: "That is why, for Christ's sake, I delight in weaknesses, in insults, in hardships, in persecutions, in difficulties. For when I am weak, then I am strong." The Spirit's empowerment for preaching is not to help us "overcome" our weaknesses to make us look strong; the Spirit empowers us in spite of our weaknesses to keep us humble and grateful and weak.

Only in our weakness do we cry out to God in desperation, as Piper explains:

> How utterly dependent we are on the Holy Spirit in
> the work of preaching! All genuine preaching is rooted
> in a feeling of desperation. You wake up on Sunday
> morning and you can smell the smoke of hell on one
> side and feel the crisp breezes of heaven on the other.
> You go to your study and look down at your pitiful

---

22. E. M. Bounds, "Prayerlessness in the Pulpit" in *E. M. Bounds on Prayer* (New Kensington, Pa.: Whitaker, 1997), 584.

manuscript, and you kneel down and cry, "God, this is so weak! Who do I think I am? What audacity to think that in three hours my words will be the odor of death to death and the fragrance of life to life (2 Cor. 2:16). My God who is sufficient for these things?"[23]

The preacher not only knows he is weak apart from the Holy Spirit; he also knows he has no message apart from God's Word. He never takes the credit or glory because he knows it belongs totally to God. The preacher knows he is a servant, not a superstar. You don't preach long before you realize how unworthy you are to be a preacher of God's holy Word. This is the burdensome angst of preaching, the fact that as preachers we feel so unworthy to preach, yet we are compelled by the Spirit to do so. The thought of preaching repels us and compels us at the same time. When we compare our own sinfulness with the sinless one of whom we preach, we are repulsed by a sense of unworthiness. Yet when the Spirit of God takes hold of us and fires us through his Word to a red-hot passion, we are compelled to preach because we see the glory of God, and we cannot keep silent; we cannot hold it in.

Hindrances to the Spirit's Empowerment

From a biblical perspective, the work of the Holy Spirit can be hindered by individuals and groups. Preachers and their churches bear a responsibility to maintain a healthy and vibrant relationship with the Holy Spirit. Paul wrote to the Thessalonians, "Do not put out the Spirit's fire" (1 Thess. 5:19). He told the Ephesians, "And do not grieve the Holy Spirit of God, with whom you were sealed for the day of redemption" (Eph. 4:30). Though I do not believe the Bible teaches we can lose the Holy Spirit, I do believe these passages warn us that sin can so harden us to the Spirit's work that we become calloused and cold toward the Spirit.

A preacher who never experiences God's power in his preaching must search himself to see if he is hindering, quenching, or putting out the Spirit's fire. York put it well when he said, "Although we cannot take credit for the power and presence of the Holy Spirit, we

---

23. Piper, *The Supremacy of God in Preaching*, 37–38.

can usually take the blame for his absence."[24] The next section of this chapter will identify the main ways we quench and grieve the Holy Spirit.

Prayerlessness. If the presence of prayer in a preacher's life indicates dependence upon God, then the absence of prayer in a preacher's life indicates independence from God. When we don't pray, we are telling God we can handle it, and we all know we cannot handle it. Prayerless preparation results in powerless preaching. Why? It has been prepared and developed in isolation from God. If only God can open the human heart to receive the Word, then we must call on him to open ours in preparation and open others in proclamation.

Fear of man. The fear of man may cause many preachers to avoid certain subjects or refrain from using the rebuking power of the Word of God. Preachers who fear men are more concerned about what people think than what God thinks about their preaching. They are more concerned about failing human expectations for their preaching than failing the Spirit's expectation for their preaching. If the Spirit's empowerment brings freedom, then the fear of man brings bondage. Preachers quench the Spirit when they fear man more than they fear God.

This quote from A. N. Martin is one of my favorite reminders that I am called to fear God alone and not man:

> The Word of God declares, "The fear of man bringeth a snare." Such fear will snare your tongue, so that when those flashes of spiritual light come to you in the pulpit, and there are applications that you know will sting and wound some choice member of the church, if your eye is to men, you will be unable to give utterance to that which you know you ought to. But when you are free from your people's smiles or frowns, you are at liberty to be an instrument of blessing to them. I submit that if there is to be increased power in the pulpit, there must be a return to the purity of motivation comprised in the fear of God.[25]

---

24. York and Decker, *Preaching with Bold Assurance,* 8.
25. A. N. Martin, *What's Wrong with Preaching Today?* (Carlisle, Pa.: Banner of Truth, 1967), 17–18.

I told you that this Martin quote was good! Keep it posted in your study and remind yourself of it often.

The preacher who wants the empowerment of the Holy Spirit must fear above all preaching in his own strength and under his own ability as well. We fear our preaching becoming filled with "wise words" because we have a little education that results in a little bigger vocabulary. We fear our preaching becoming manipulative because we know how to hold an audience and work a crowd. We fear that people will put their trust or their confidence in us because they think we are "good." We fear preaching that depends more on our talents as communicators than it does on the power of the Holy Spirit to change lives.

Pride. One of the reasons preachers fear people is their own pride. The preacher who is wrapped up in himself seeks to have his ego stroked by the affirmation of others. He craves the spotlight of the platform and is never satisfied unless he is the center of attention. The problem is that the Spirit's witness is to Christ, not the preacher. Stott wrote:

> Why, then, does the power of the Spirit seem to accompany our preaching so seldom? I strongly suspect that the main reason is our pride. In order to be filled with the Spirit, we have first to acknowledge our own emptiness. In order to be exalted and used by God, we have first to humble ourselves under his mighty hand.[26]

Sin. A preacher can also forfeit God's empowering presence by rebelling against God's standard for Christian living. I am talking about the impurity of the mind and heart. Preachers who live in disobedience lack the holiness that the Spirit desires. Sometimes we want the Spirit's empowerment, but we forget the first part of his name is Holy. Preaching dirty never invites the Spirit's empowerment. If a preacher will not hear and heed the Spirit's conviction in his quiet time, he should not expect the Spirit to show up at preaching time.

Calling. One sure way to miss the Spirit's empowerment in your preaching is to miss the Spirit's call on your life. Preachers who run like Jonah from God's will soon find themselves struggling outside

---

26. John R. W. Stott, *Between Two Worlds: The Art of Preaching in the Twentieth Century* (Grand Rapids: Eerdmans, 1982), 329–30.

God's will. If you preach without calling—that is, if you preach without first being authorized by God to preach—you preach in your own power, not God's. You must be sure of your initial call to preach the gospel; but you must be equally sure that you are exercising his call exactly where God wants you to be. The minute you begin to doubt whether you are where you are supposed to be, you open yourself up to all kinds of doubts, misgivings, and second-guessing. William Still elaborates:

> The man who knows Christ and is called to be a prophet may yet find the Holy Ghost "desert" him because he is preaching out of turn or without specific commission. He may be preaching in the wrong place, or from the wrong motive, or the wrong message. He may be powerless for no other reason than that he is not in God's appointment. He may have left his God-given post for personal or domestic reasons, to please his wife or educate his children or to escape persecutors. Though none of these are trivial reasons, if they do not please God, he certainly cannot bless disobedience and has promised, "if ye forsake him, he will forsake you."[27]

Impure motives. Study Paul's preaching, and you will immediately discover how important purity of motive is. He told the Thessalonians his preaching did not come from impure motives (1 Thess. 2:3). He told the Corinthians he was not after their money or possessions (2 Cor. 12:14). He said in Acts 24:16 that he always strove to keep his conscience clear before man and God. Check your heart often and ask yourself why you are preaching the gospel. Preach for any motive other than the glory of God, and the Spirit will not empower such preaching.

Lack of preparation. We may also grieve the Spirit through neglect. We are so busy that we have little time to pay attention to the spiritual dynamics of preaching, much less put together a coherent message for Sunday. To wake up Sunday after Sunday begging the Spirit to forgive our laziness, our lack of self-control, and our consummation with worldly things and then to ask him to

---

27. William Still, "Preaching and the Holy Spirit," *Christianity Today,* 2 September 1957, 10.

bless our sermons is hypocritical and presumptive. This should not be, brothers! Waiting until the last minute to call on the Spirit is not a demonstration of faith; it's a demonstration of how lightly we take our preaching and our need for the Holy Spirit. He is the God-sent Paraclete who lives inside you, not a switch you turn on and off on Sundays when you need a little boost in the pulpit.

Lack of belief. The preacher who never thinks about or longs for the Spirit's empowering presence in his preaching has no reason to expect it. I am talking about more than a name-it-and-claim-it desire. I am talking about a burden that comes from within, that keeps us on our knees and keenly aware of the Spirit's leadership in our preaching. Spurgeon is said to have so desired the Spirit's power in his preaching that on each step up to his elevated pulpit he said to himself, "I believe in the power of the Holy Ghost." He expected it and he anticipated it.

Though it is beyond the scope of this chapter, let me at least acknowledge that openness to the empowerment of the Holy Spirit in preaching does not imply that you must also be open to speaking in tongues or other signs and wonders. Furthermore, being open to the biblical ministry of the Holy Spirit's illumination does not imply that we must follow illuminism, which is the idea that the subjective visions and experiences one has outside of Christ and Scripture are necessary and desired for spirituality. Instead, I am simply calling pastors and preachers to take a hard look at the biblical ministry of the Holy Spirit and his relationship to the preaching of the Word of God. If our generation is to see a movement of God on the scale of the Great Awakenings, we must return to the passion and the fervency of the Holy Spirit accompanied by the power of the Word of God in our preaching.

Lack of preaching Jesus. One of the greatest ways to quench the Spirit's empowerment is to talk about everything under the sun except the Son. I tell my students each semester that they have a choice to make when they preach: they can make much of Jesus, or they can make much of themselves. But they cannot do both at the same time. The Spirit's empowerment for preaching is tied to our character, for sure. But it is also tied to our content as well. Close the Bible, don't mention Jesus Christ, and preach your feelings and opinions about the events, politics, and culture of the day; and the Spirit will evacuate what you are calling a sermon. Open the Bible, honor the Spirit's inspiration, lift up Christ from the passage you are preaching, and the Spirit will lift up the message you are preaching.

The Spirit's Empowerment: Frequency or Intensity

How frequently should we expect the Spirit's empowering presence to show up in our preaching? Once in a lifetime? Once a year? Once a month? Once a week? I think we should expect the Spirit's power to move us, the message, and the people we preach to into the presence of God every time we preach. If my life is Spirit led, and if my preparation is Spirit led, then I believe my presentation will be Spirit demonstrated. As preachers, we all experience varying degrees of intensity of the Spirit's empowerment. Sometimes his presence is undeniably strong, his influence on the congregation is visible, and we sense God moving. At other times the Spirit is working more quietly, behind the scenes, in a less visible or noticeable way.

So instead of thinking in terms of frequency, I think the better approach is to think of the Spirit's working in terms of intensity. The more sensitive we are to the Spirit's presence, the more intense we will perceive his work. The more distracted or preoccupied we are with others things, the less intense that perception will be.

Conclusion

As I bring this chapter and this book to a close, I am having the same feeling in my heart that I do when I preach. I am thankful and grateful for the opportunity to preach, but I never quite feel like I do the text justice. I could have said more. I could have brought up additional insights. It's what I call the "shoulda, coulda, woulda" effect. Perhaps it's the Spirit's way to keep us hungry for more. The Spirit says to us, "You cannot drain the significance and the beauty of my inspired text. You cannot eat it all in one sitting. I will keep you coming back to the table to feast on more of my Word." And so it is with the Spirit's empowerment for preaching. So this is not an ending but a beginning, as you seek to examine and implement a more Spirit-led approach in your own preaching. My prayer is that the Spirit used this book to start a new work in your life—a fresh and continual dependence upon the Holy Spirit.

As you approach your preaching ministry in the days ahead, may God burn this verse upon your heart and mind and continually bring you back to this truth: "'Not by might nor by power, but by my Spirit,' says the LORD Almighty" (Zech. 4:6).

Index